The Puzzle of Humanity

Carl du Prel

The Puzzle of Humanity

*An Introduction to the Study
of the Occult Sciences*

Carl du Prel

translated by Kerry A Nitz

K A Nitz
AUCKLAND, NEW ZEALAND

ISBN: 978-0-473-63520-6

Foreword

The present text arose out of two lectures which were held in Munich and then published in the magazine "Sphinx" (V. 366–376; VI. 31–39; XIII. 49–55; 161–170; 216–224). Here they are expanded and fused together. But I would like this "Introduction to the Study of the Occult Sciences" not just perhaps to be heeded by opponents, but rather by also by adherents; for there is no less sinning within the walls of Troy than there is outside them. It is even a common error of opponents as of adherents that they see the resurgence of the occult sciences as a reactionary phenomenon.

First of all concerning the opponents, they consider the achievements of modern science to be endangered and believe they are seeing the wild superstitions of past cultural epochs emerging again. If now the phenomena to which the occult sciences relate were inseparable from their medieval explanation, if the occult sciences were being resurrected *along with this explanation*, then we would admittedly be taking a backward step. If we would see in all somnambulists only the possessed, in all mediums only witches and sorcerers who have through a pact with Satan come into the possession of their abnormal powers and abilities, then admittedly the modern mysticism would be a reactionary phenomenon. But such explanations are no longer worth mentioning. The question of fact has simply been posed anew as to whether the phenomena of the occult sciences exist at all, a question which was overhastily answered in the negative by the superficial period of the Enlightenment. That in fact was the error of that Enlightenment, that they considered the phenomena to be inseparable from their explanation at the time — since you now objected to the explanation, you believed you had eliminated the facts with it, that is, you emptied the baby out with the bathwater. It is essential to avoid this error today, and if it is to be avoided, then the appearance of reaction will also disappear. The Pythia in Delphi was regarded in ancient times to be inspired by Apollo, in the Middle Ages she would have been exorcised as someone possessed, today she would be defined as a somnambulist. The facts remain and only the explanations change.

Now it cannot be denied, however, that even the adherents of the occult sciences often only get a reactionary understanding from this. In particular the number of those spiritualists is considerable who think that with the belief in the immortality of the soul the entire church faith will now also be revived again with all its orthodox limitations. But the belief in immortality of the soul has already found a place in the various religious systems, has thus not grown together inseparably with any of them. Thus this part of the church faith can very well find its new foundation without it being necessary to accept the entire system in which it is found to be integrated.

The occult sciences in their modern form should not at all lead to a faith, but rather prepare a new knowledge, and already as a result they point not back into the past, but rather far out into the future. They are competent, for the world view of the future which already shows itself in the process of forming, of delivering that very important component which concerns the solution of the puzzle of humanity. Once completed, this world view will reveal its great significance in that it will stand there as the synthesis of religion and science, of metaphysics and natural history. It will not address itself one-sidedly to the human heart, like religion, but also not one-sidedly to the mind, like science. It will not be religion of blind faith ossified in dogma, but will also not be like that science from whose chairs today an ice-cold breeze wafts onto the life of the people. As metaphysics it will not merely move in conceptual constructions, but rather like the natural sciences have a foundation in the facts of experience which can even be researched experimentally.

Despite all the lack of clarity which the present fermentation process brings with itself, the ground lines of that future world view can — which the present text shall show — already be drafted today to the extent that they betray the form of a closed system. This world view will not be limited to a caste of scholars, like our present-day philosophy, but rather it will stand in close connection with our cultural life; because in it people will receive a new and deepened definition, they will logically also make out new purposes of existence and new goals of human striving. A long way from being reactionary, it is thus competent instead to rejuvenate our entire cultural life.

Munich, in April 1892.

Dr Carl du Prel.

The Puzzle of Humanity

To what extent is the human a puzzle? At least it is in so far as physiology and physiological psychology are still immature sciences. But of *that* less shall be spoken here than of that puzzle rather which will still remain when those sciences have been completed. It would be quite interesting if we already today knew exactly what the human is in physical respects; but even then precisely the key questions would remain unanswered: From where do we come? What do we live for? To where are we going?

You could say — and many say it — that these problems do not exist at all; in the following it will appear, however, that they are admittedly a given. If they are not given, however, then they also urgently demand their solution, and indeed from various causes of which, however, that of the egotistic interest alone would be sufficient to bring us to attention. In addition it must be described as a scientific scandal that the human who forms the pinnacle of the earthly creation is not even clear about himself. We have the advantage of self-awareness over the animals; but we can boast little about it so long as our self is a puzzle to us.

How does it come about now, however, that our self-awareness is too small a light to illuminate the puzzle of our self? In order to answer this question, we must return to the cause of our existence, but stand immediately before three diametrically opposed views — the materialist, the pantheistic, and the mystical. According to the materialist view, our existence begins with our birth, and the tiny luminosity of self-awareness has biological and physiological causes; the earthly dead and blind material shall have developed entirely by itself — but don't ask me how — as far as perception and consciousness, and shall rise still further in the biological process; the current degree of development, however, does not suffice to solve the puzzle of humanity. The pantheistic view has us go forth from a metaphysical world substance which is indeed also blind, but has an urge though to come to knowledge of itself, and to this end puts a spotlight on the world process; this inward contemplation of God reaches its current highest state in the human brain, but is yet in a bad way since the light proves to be too little. Quite different is the mystical view; with this our birth is not the beginning of our existence, but rather our earthly life is preceded by a quite different, individual existence which we forget though at birth. Accordingly the smallness of our self-awareness would be explicable by the diminution occurring at birth.

If we now compare these three views, many will thus say that the materialistic is plausible and clear, the pantheistic harder to think and quite opaque, the mystical though quite unthinkable and entirely opaque. So it is, however, only in appearance; in reality it is in fact reversed. Materialism is admittedly clear, but only because it is superficial, doing entirely without metaphysical insight. Pantheism is much deeper, but has the disadvantage of never being able to be proved by facts, and must always only remain speculation. In contrast, clarity without superficiality attaches in fact to the seemingly so opaque mystical view, and since it can also be proven by the facts of experience, it would long since have been accepted if attention had been paid to these facts.

But these facts shall yet be spoken of. Firstly, however, a simple comparison shall introduce the reader to the mystical view and demonstrate that the smallness of our self-awareness could in fact be the result of a diminution. This comparison does not indeed explain, but proves at the least its psychological possibility.

Let us think of the following case. On a ship which is sailing in the Pacific Ocean, a sailor is put into a hypnotic trance and receives the suggestion of continuing to sleep until evening, but to then awaken without any recollection of his past. After this suggestion is impressed firmly on him, the sailor is carried down onto a boat and marooned on a small island in the ocean; the ship heading off though at full sail.

After awakening now, this sailor would be perfectly like a new-born human, with the difference only that he would come into his world as a fully developed and intelligent being; he would begin his existence as a man. But he would ponder quite in vain over who he was and how he came into this nature that was completely foreign to him. Without any memory of his past, he would be astonished, indeed shocked over himself and the place where he awoke to a degree that he could easily become melancholic.

The ocean stretches as far as his eyes can see — an image the like of which he believes he has never seen. He turns inland to orient himself to his island, but everything appears unfamiliar to him; he does not recall ever seeing things of this sort — plants and animals, mountains and the clouds which pass over them. Finally he sees also beings of his likeness; he hurries to them in order to receive information from them; but they are all in the same incomprehensible state; they do not know who they are, nor from where they come.

A society in such a strange state would consume itself in brooding over itself and its island; but all that reflection and mutual questioning would not cast light on the unfathomable fatefulness by virtue of which they are there. With a mixture of high admiration and astonishment, they would see as a spectacle never seen before the sun setting, covering the ocean with a bridge of flooding golden light, and their astonishment would be boundless in turn when thousands of stars began to burgeon in the dark sky.

With time the bodily needs would certainly divert them from their brooding. Hunger and thirst, exhaustion and sleep arrive; the rigours of the weather require that they look around for shelter, and thus the strange Robinsonade on this island would commence, which makes you think; for Robinson brought his cultural memories with him to his island, whilst our island residents would have to devise and invent everything anew.

It is not necessary to describe this situation any further, and also whether a hypnotic emptying out of the brain can go so far — experiments of a similar sort have indeed been made — that the awakening from sleep would amount entirely to a rebirth does not concern us here. I have nevertheless not spoken of entirely imaginary things — the island which is under consideration is called the earth; the ocean which flows around it is called space; the beings which meet on the island are called humans, and the protracted Robinsonade which they are performing is called the cultural history of humanity.

In fact, if we think with some circumspection about our own earthly position, the comparison with those island residents is justified on all points, with the exception of one only — we do not awaken with developed consciousness as mature beings, but rather with undeveloped consciousness as helpless creatures. Since this is the only difference, it can also only lie on this one point that we behave in a completely different way to those island residents. They awaken as contemplative philosophers; for a philosopher is anyone who is capable of wondering over their existence and that of the world. We, on the other hand, become accustomed in the course of childhood to the look of things and our own existence so much that they, far from making us dismayed, appear to us as comprehensible in themselves. When our consciousness has reached its maturity, it has by the deadening power of habit become incapable of astonishment, and thus we are absorbed during our life entirely in practical activities. Sometimes certainly the incomprehensibility of our situation comes into the consciousness of the more reflective among us, and both puzzles, world and humanity, become objects worthy of meditation by founders of religions and by philosophers, indeed they are declared to be the most important objects with which the human mind or spirit can occupy itself; but their endeavours to bring us to our senses have never obtained deep and lasting influence because they themselves do not agree on the solution to both puzzles.

At any rate, everywhere and always, if not the clear realisation, then the dark feeling in humanity shows that there is something extremely strange about the human and his place in the world. It has never wanted to appear understandable entirely by itself to humanity that we find ourselves on this cosmic island without knowing to where or why. Already our urge to orient ourselves better to our island does not correspond to merely practical needs, but rather also to an objective interest and the hope of perhaps also solving in this way our own puzzle; but the founders of religions and the philosophers emphasise again and again that we will not obtain any clarity with mere natural science expeditions on our island, that rather behind all physics something else must yet lie, a metaphysics, and only there lies the solving of the puzzle.

Cultural epochs often occur in which the belief in metaphysics is accepted on all sides, indeed even obtains fixed forms. But again and again come periods of doubt not merely in these forms, but rather in the problem itself. Then that strange head sickness occurs which Schopenhauer named the metaphysical humbleness, and which often occurred epidemically and went on for a long time. Anyone then who still retained however much capability for astonishment and circumspection passed for a dreamer and self-torturer. In our day this sickness has even taken on the form of a scientific system which is called materialism. The materialists are so-to-say thought abstainers; they claim with great definiteness that nothing at all preceded our arrival on the island, and our departure from it, death, will be followed by nothing; also no puzzle of humanity exists at all, for we are products of the island itself, and made entirely of the same material as it is. Now this material had risen up by its own power into organic material — the way Baron Münchhausen pulled himself out of the morass by his own hair — and thus even life and thinking become in the end characteristics of the material.

The world is a physical problem to the materialist, the human a chemical problem. That they now are certainly in fact, but that does not hinder that they are at the same time metaphysical problems. Were the world to be explained to the last star as a physical problem entirely and to the smallest detail, we would thus stand before such an astonishing thing that any circumspect person would then come straightaway to a consciousness of the metaphysical problem, like that Indian king who kept many scholars at his court who had to come to him sometimes and lecture; they knew how to talk about everything excellently, about what and how, but could not satisfy the king, and when they were finished, he concluded the discussion every time with the question, "Yes, why then is there anything at all?" But his scholars never knew an answer to that.

The materialist sees in the world only the mechanical side, and because he only recognises powers working in accordance with natural law, all of nature seems to him to be a play without aim or purpose. Neither the world, nor our own existence have a purpose for him. Mechanical conformity to natural laws and unreasoning purposelessness are identical concepts to him. This is the foundational idea of materialism, but also its fundamental error; for purposes can very well be obtained and will very frequently be reached by way of a mechanism in accordance with natural laws. In such cases the suitability for purpose is even all the more indisputable and all the more perfect, the more perfect the mechanism is. With our pocket watches, with every technical invention, the mechanism is wound in service to a purpose; the same could thus very well apply to the world.

The natural sciences' definition of the thing only ever concerns the outside, not the essence. Goethe's Faust can be dissolved in terms of the natural sciences into paper made from rags along with printing ink; an aria by Mozart can in terms of the natural sciences be explained as a series of sequential vibrations in the air. But Goethe and Mozart would think twice if such a definition were held to be exhaustive; and likewise the more circumspect amongst us have since time immemorial thought twice about considering the explanation of the natural sciences for the world to be exhaustive. The world is quite indisputably a natural sciences' problem, but next to that still an aesthetic, ethical, and metaphysical problem. That is something acknowledged since time immemorial by everyone whose mind does not remain fastened to the surface of things.

Certainly it is the more difficult piece of work which yet remains for the natural sciences. Those island residents mentioned at the beginning would still have done very little for the resolution of their situation if they had just researched their island thoroughly. Humanity, however, has not yet even achieved this regarding the world.

Our knowledge is piecemeal. The empirical sciences which we pursue are very far from being concluded, and it is above all certain that ever new branches of knowledge will arise. There can thus also for the present still be no talk of our philosophy, our world view somehow being complete. That is even less the case when precisely the natural phenomena most important for the foundation of a world view are particularly opaque and puzzling for us. Astronomy encompasses the largest piece of the world and has experienced the most exact development; but with the discovery of the merely external natural stage little is served philosophically, and in the viewing of the stars we only experience impressions which remain more or less in the sphere of sensation, whereby the world remains, however, only a great question mark. When we limit our view, however, to the earth, we are no less troubled by it. In mineralogy, for example, most of it is clear, but we cannot draw philosophical gains from it. In biology by contrast, which is far more important, it teems with puzzles. The human, however, the highest of all natural facts, is at the same time the greatest of all puzzles. Not even by his physiological side is he entirely comprehensible; psychology though, which busies itself with his highest functions, is so much the battle place of opinions that opposed definitions of humanity exist. For the one we are a house of chemicals, for the other an emanation of God.

Now the fate of all philosophy, however, depends to a certain extent on psychology; for as the human can be explained sufficiently only from his highest functions, so nature only from its highest phenomenon, and that is just again the human which forms the flower at least of the nature known to us. The philosophy thus which pursues metaphysics without previously getting the psychology right would be like a botanist who wanted to ignore the fruit in the explanation of a fruit tree.

The facts of nature are irrevocably not of equal value for the explanation of the world, and they are unfortunately all the more opaque, the more important they are. We must thus postpone the attempt to solve the world puzzle until we have first solved the puzzle of humanity, and indeed quite especially the psychological side of it, that is, the puzzle of the human soul. Now the greatest minds have admittedly busied themselves with it from time immemorial, but how little has yet been achieved is shown by the fact that the contrast between materialism and spiritualism is still as sharp today as in antiquity, indeed even sharper because both parties are attaining ever more precise expressions of their key point and its substantiation. Many sceptics have already concluded from this futility of the long dispute that the soul belongs to the unsolvable problems by which it is not just termed "ignoramus" [we do not know], but rather "ignorabimus" [we will not know].

Should we now really throw in the towel? I do not believe so. A definitive abandonment would only be advisable if it were proven that the solution has been sought for on the right path and all means have been exhausted already. But as soon as it is proven — and that shall happen here — that a false path has been adopted and the most significant aids for solving the problem have not yet been attempted at all, we will shake off the present lethargy and obtain fresh courage to take up the work of inquiry again. But it must admittedly be said here already that in the pointing out of the correct way our insight that human knowledge is only piecemeal will yet receive a much deeper foundation that it was previously given. But when it is also shown that the problem lies much deeper than previously guessed, we will likewise be better for it than our predecessors because it will at least be clear at what points the lever is to be applied.

It is quite comprehensible that one took as the starting point for the inquiry into the problem of the soul that which was known to us about humanity; in other words, that one analysed the content of human self-awareness in order to find the soul. One considered it obvious that the learning about souls and the analysis of consciousness were identical concepts. And yet that was only a petitio principii [begging of the question], an unproven assumption. It could indeed at any rate be — the logic at least has no objection to this hypothesis — that the soul would not be found at all in our self-awareness, that the light of our self knowledge did not at all reach down into the depths of our nature. But it is also thinkable that the material in the way of facts on whose foundation a theory of souls is to be erected had not been sufficiently researched, indeed that precisely the decisive facts had been ignored.

It is not difficult to show that in fact both reservations are justified — one has searched for the soul in the wrong place, and has in the right place ignored the decisive facts.

That the soul does not lie at all in our self-awareness, but rather outside it, that thus the theory of souls went amiss right at the outset, is indisputable. For what is our self-awareness? Obviously only a special case of consciousness, from which it is not distinguished by the organ, but rather by the object. Self-awareness is the consciousness directed inwardly, to our own self. But what is consciousness? It is a biological product of development. Biology shows that the development of consciousness goes parallel with the increase and intensification of the organisation. The most complicated living being, the human, is at the same time in possession of the most developed consciousness. But even with humanity consciousness is not a finished product; it is not a match for its object, the world, it lags behind its object. Already the view of the starry heavens teaches us that our knowledge is to what we do not know as a drop is to the ocean. Only a tiny part of that which is arrives through the channels of our senses into our consciousness. Our senses are limited not only in number, but rather every single one is limited in relation to its performance. Our eyes are only equipped for the seven colour spectrum, for the colours of the rainbow; but the spectrum has on this side, as on that, an additional piece of indeterminate extent. There are infrared and ultraviolet rays; such as are based on a too large and others on a too small number of oscillations in the ether to be visible. Such rays are verified by physical apparatuses which are more sensitive than the retina. In a similar way, all our senses are limited. Oscillations in the air which are based on fewer than 30 or more than 24 thousand oscillations a second make no sound for us.

There are furthermore forces in nature which do not correspond to any human sense at all, and only become discernable in that they transform themselves into other forces. We have no sense for magnetic or electrical processes. Finally, however, it must also be mentioned that we do not perceive at all the objective processes of nature, but rather only their effect on us; not oscillations in the ether, but rather light; not oscillations in the air, but rather sounds. We thus have as it were a subjectively falsified image of the world; only that does not affect our orientation because this falsification is not individual and runs in a constant manner governed by rules.

Those are just sentences which are to be proven by the natural sciences in an exact manner. The natural sciences thus suffice already in themselves for contradicting materialism. Materialism stands and falls with the claim that only the sensory is real. We have five senses; thus — so concludes the materialist — material has five characteristics. With such logic you could just as well say there is no sun because there are blind people. Materialism has also as natural science itself proven that the world extends beyond our senses; it has undermined its own foundations; it has sawed off the branch on which it was itself sitting. As philosophy, however, it claims to still sit up above. Materialism thus has no right at all to call itself a world view; it does not extend to it at all, and it is delusions of grandeur when it calls itself a philosophy. It has only the entitlement of a branch of knowledge, and in addition the world, the object of its study, is world of mere appearance, and to want to build a world view on that is an obvious contradiction. The real world is something different, qualitatively and quantitatively, from the one that materialism knows, and only the real world can be the object of a philosophy.

What now applies to consciousness, that it lags behind its object, must also apply to self-awareness as a mere special case of consciousness and indeed to a heightened degree. For firstly the object of self-awareness is a much more mysterious structure than any one thing in the world known to us; and furthermore, however, the consciousness as it were is preceded already by a long biological development history, so that it forms a perhaps already quite high rung of the ladder; in contrast, a self-awareness, or at least an actual self-knowledge is only worth speaking of with *humanity*; it thus forms the first rung, is only given in its first stage. It is thus only the more probably that it does not exhaust its object, our selves. With that, however, judgement is pronounced on that psychology which wants to limit itself to mere analysis of self-awareness; it contradicts the theory of development and it comprehends itself that the problem cannot be solved in this way.

20

Self-awareness does not even illuminate the physical side of our nature completely. As our threshold of sensation cuts us off from the external processes of nature — over whose number and composition we cannot even make guesses — so too for the processes within us. The organic functions, growth, nourishment, digestion, heart activity, etc. run in the healthy body unconsciously. According to the old theory of souls, these functions would belong to material foreign to our bodies, with which the soul had been coupled by virtue of an inexplicable fate. It could, however, at any rate be that these organic functions notwithstanding their conformity to natural laws belonged though to our own nature. We need only again let drop the false assumption that the nature of the soul lies in consciousness; it could indeed also be the animating and organising principle, and then the unconsciousness of the organic functions would still be no proof for the foreign source of them. If these too were taken care of by the soul, then the human would be explained uniformly.

Even in our purely psychological functions, in feelings, thoughts, and acts of will, we do not yet grasp the entire nature of our souls. The materialists even claim that too, in that only the nature of our body is covered, that also thoughts and feelings are only functions of the body. Now it is admittedly illogical and only even with the materialists very common to transform the *cum hoc* [with this] into a *propter hoc* [because of this]; but it is indisputable at any rate that thoughts and feelings are bound to bodily organs, and run in parallel with bodily states. On that precisely rests the plausibility of the materialism which concludes from this parallelism that there are no souls at all. But we do not need to get drawn at all into this point of the dispute. The dispute, however, over whether this being bound comprises a mere relationship of coordination — as the spiritualists say — or a relationship of causality — as the materialists claim — is already as old as psychology itself. We can, however, let it rest entirely since we will obtain the proof of souls from quite different, much more conclusive facts, namely from such as with which there is no talk of being bound to the bodily organs.

In accordance with the aforementioned, we thus place this sentence at the top: the soul does not lie in the circle of illumination of our self-awareness, it lies in the unconscious.

Here the sceptic could now immediately be tempted to respond: if the soul lies in the unconscious, then it cannot also be drawn forth from it, the question of souls must thus be put aside until the onset of a biological deepening of the self-awareness. But the matter does not stand so poorly. If the functions of the soul are unconscious to us in respect to the process, much of the result falls in our consciousness, as we will yet see. It is in respect to the life of our minds* a quite constant phenomenon that the unconscious and consciousness are only alternately shown to their advantage. Already with the production of genius we see the veiling, in hypnotism, however, even the suppression of sensory consciousness as a condition of such phenomena which belong to the unconscious; the awakening without memory is a further proof for this opposition.

This opposition proves now indisputably a dualism within the life of our minds, and thus we find ourselves immediately placed before the important question of whether only a dualism within the life of the brain is present, or perhaps a dualism of brain and soul. In the first case, a double ego would be expected whose *both* halves were embraced by physiological psychology; in the second case, by contrast, we would have to acknowledge that definition of the human which Kant already drew up a hundred years ago — a subject which divides into two persons. One of these persons would thereby be of physiological nature, the other of psychological. Whether now this definition is correct depends entirely on whether all activity of the mind or spirit is bound to the life of the brain, or whether also enticed out from the unconscious are such functions which differentiate themselves from the *toto genere* [whole family] of those bound to the brain, for which we must

---

*   [Tr.: the German word *Geistesleben* means life of the *Geist*, where *Geist* in this context can mean *mind, intellect,* or *spirit.* Thus *Geist* combines the concepts of mind and spirit in a way that is more difficult to express in English. This should be taken into consideration where you see *life of our minds* in this text.]

thus assume a different organ. Only in this last case would we have found in the unconscious a soul.

The Kantian definition of the human has remained without influence on psychology because the science neglects that factual material which forms the empirical foundation for this definition — and which unfortunately was unknown in Kant's time — right up to today in an irresponsible way. These facts which it deals with form the object of the occult sciences which are, as is well-known, still the Cinderella today.

The failure in the question of souls lies thus in fact in both the circumstances mentioned above — at first one sought the soul in the wrong place, in consciousness instead of in the unconscious; but then, when one — and also even recently — drew the unconscious into research, one emphasised in the right place the wrong facts, namely those which prove an unconscious life of the brain, but not those which prove a life of the soul next to the life of the brain.

Anyone who acknowledges the facts of the occult sciences thus finds themselves referred back to the Kantian definition of the human. He does not accept it arbitrarily, but rather of necessity. He will then say — which the occult sciences prove — that our soul life *lies* for our earthly consciousness in the unconscious, but that the soul *is* in no way an unconscious; that its functions become evident alternately with the conscious functions; that these functions are distinguished from the conscious according to their entire quality, and that they become unconscious to us again with the return of sensory consciousness.

With that a real duality of our nature is given, a duality of soul and brain — whose monistic dissolution will yet occupy us — not merely a dualism within the life of the brain. The consciousness, bound to the senses and the brain as organ, would then only comprise one half of our nature — the earthly phenomenon; but from this another half of our nature is to be distinguished which may for the time being be described as the supersensory.

Thus the soul then really lies much deeper than has previously been supposed, and it turns out that a real psychology is yet to be written. But at least we know now the place where the soul is to be found, and have the prospect of inferring its existence and composition from such functions which indisputably can only belong to it, which are not bound to any bodily organ, from which thus the materialistic moaner will keep his distance. Considered in itself, that theory of souls whose main features Kant described appears as an extremely hopeless undertaking; but if we view the facts on which it is to be erected as foundation, it turns out that this new theory of souls not only has more prospects of reaching its goal than the old one, but rather that only it can reach it at all.

Kant said, "I confess that I am very inclined to claim the existence of immaterial natures in the world and to place my soul itself in the class of these natures." In consideration, however, of the simultaneous material nature of humans, he continues, "The human soul would hence already have to be seen in the present life as associated with two worlds at the same time, from which it, provided it is bound to a personal unit with a body, feels the material world alone clearly. [...] It is therefore one and the same subject which belongs as a part to the visible and invisible world at the same time, but not even the same person, because the ideas of one, on account of their different composition, are not concomitant ideas from that of the other world, and hence what I think as spirit is not acknowledged by me as a human, and vice versa."*

Now there are admittedly people who say Kant's "Träume eines Geistersehers" [Dreams of a Visionary] is only a satire on Swedenborg and the belief in spirits. This view, however, is completely contradicted by the fact that Kant 22 years later held lectures in which he expressed entirely the same views and indeed again in connection to Swedenborg whose ideas he called "sublime".† Incidentally the claim also thereby becomes invalid that Kant only flirted with the world of spirits in his precritical period. I have — because it is not found in any complete edition – newly published the most important

---

*   Immanuel Kant, "Träume eines Geistersehers, erläutert durch Träume der Metaphysik," in Immanuel Kant's vermischte Schriften, vol. 2 (Halle: Regersche Buchhandlung, 1799), 266, 275, 285.

†   Immanuel Kant, Immanuel Kant's Vorlesungen über die Metaphysik: nebst einer Einleitung, welche eine kurze Uebersicht der wichtigsten Veränderungen der Metaphysik seit Kant enthält, ed. Karl Heinrich Ludwig Pölitz (Erfurt: Keysersche Buchhandlung, 1821).

part of those lectures in which Kant shows himself to be a mystic within the critical period, and want to provide a few remarks from it:

> Life consists in the commerce of the soul with the body; the beginning of life is the beginning of the commerce, the end of life is the end of the commerce. The beginning of the commerce is the birth, the end of the commerce is the death. The duration of the commerce is the life. The beginning of life is the birth; *this is, however, not the beginning of the life of the soul, but rather that of the human.* The end of life is the death; *this is, however, not the end of the life of the soul, but rather of the human.* Birth, life, and death are thus only *conditions* of the soul. [...] Therefore the substance remains even though the body passes away, and thus the substance must also have been there when the body arose. [...] Life with the human is twofold — the animal and the spirit life. The animal life is the life of the human as human; and with this the body is necessary so that the human lives. The other life is the spirit life where the soul, independent of the body, must continue to exercise the same acts of life.*

As you see, Kant's theory of souls contains all necessary components. He teaches that the soul lies in the unconscious, and the simultaneity of both persons of our subject; he teaches furthermore pre-existence and immortality. But without worrying about that, the later psychology has only again researched the one person of our nature which begins with birth and ends with death, and on *this* path the theory of souls must admittedly have led to materialism.

Kant was, however, also clear over it being the occult sciences on which the theory of souls had to be erected. Just for that reason he linked up with a visionary, with Swedenborg, which admittedly did not turn out entirely to his satisfaction. But we with incomparably richer factual material can expand

---

*   Immanuel Kant, Vorlesungen über Psychologie: Mit einer Einleitung: Kants mystische Weltanschauung, ed. Carl du Prel (Leipzig: Ernst Günther, 1889), 75, 76, 79.

the theory of souls in Kant's sense. For apart from that antiquity and the Middle Ages have provided us with rich treasures — only for our science to not trouble itself with them — we have had for 100 years somnambulism, for 50 years hypnotism, and for 40 years spiritualism.

But in order to be on the safe side with the utilisation of them, we must in advance realise what it was that science rightly objected to in the old theory of souls, what mistakes are thus to be avoided in the new.

The old theory of souls is dualistic; it puts the human together from a mortal body and an immortal soul without being able to explain their connection. Science, however, desires rightly a monistic explanation of the human. The old theory of souls sought the soul in self-awareness; in it we find, however, only such mental functions as are bound to bodily organs, senses, and the brain, and then it very much suggests itself to materialism to make the brain as the cause of thought and to set up the unprovable sentence: matter thinks. The soul was then absolutely superfluous. This is admittedly a monism, but not a provable one.

Now, however, a monism, and indeed a provable one, would also then be established if the body and the bodily associated spirit, instead of being derived from one another, succeeded in being derived from a common third, the soul. That now is what the new theory of souls does; it is monistic and has the advantage of allocating the soul to the right place, namely the unconscious. It is not the brain that thinks, but rather the soul thinks through the brain. Something quite analogous happens in the activity of the senses — the feelings are produced first in the brain. The eyes do not see, but rather they only gather the impressions and deliver them to the brain where they are transformed into perceptions. Seeing is an intellectual act; the brain sees through the eyes. And likewise the soul thinks through the brain.

This monism has considerable advantages over the materialistic monism. Materialism explains reason out of the irrational, thinking out of the blind, life out of dead matter. But it is entirely illogical to infer from the highest functions of the human, reason and morality, the lowest principle, matter. You cannot infer from a clock ticking well a bad clockmaker.

If the function of the brain is rational, then obviously the organ must also be derived from a somehow rational cause. That is what the new theory of souls does; it has the materialistic idea that the brain produces the thoughts apply up to a certain degree, but it adds that the soul produces the brain.

In order to do justice to all demands, the new theory of souls must also explain the connection of the soul to the body. To this end we need only extend the just mentioned relationship existing between the brain and soul to the entire body, that is, we must ascribe to the soul the ability to organise by virtue of which it is capable of forming the body. Not just the brain, but rather the entire body is the organ of the soul. If we assume this demand to be resolved — it should occupy us immediately — then with it admittedly the unconscious would not yet be transformed into a soul, but rather only into a blind organising will. If we in addition ascribe to this will also the capability for imagination and knowledge, obviously under proof of credentials — that should also happen. — is then the unconscious transformed into a soul?

Still not. Rather we have merely taken the step from Schopenhauer to Hartmann. With Schopenhauer the unconscious is a blind will, with Hartmann it has will *and* imagination. Schopenhauer has merely overcome materialism; but for explaining the puzzle of humanity his blind will does not suffice. A blind will cannot light the lamp of knowledge; it cannot build the brain as the organ of rational thought. Hence Hartmann is right to ascribe the imagination to the unconscious; but even for him the soul slips between his fingers in that he does a somersault and identifies the unconscious with the world substance. With that the blind panthelism* of Schopenhauer is indeed overcome, but not pantheism.

A theory of souls calling itself so with right must not only furnish proof of a metaphysical essence in humans — as Schopenhauer and Hartmann did — but rather a metaphysical *individuality*. When this demand is also satisfied — and that too should happen — only then would we have an actual soul. This would lie in the unconscious, but would not itself

---

*   [Tr.: Panthelism = Schopenhauer's theory that the ultimate reality of the universe is will.]

be unconscious, but rather would have will and cognition and an individuality. Thus only then would our unconscious be transformed into a soul, into a subject.

In order now to preserve this subject from the confusion with the person of the earthly consciousness, that is, in order to emphasise the difference with the old theory of souls which commits this mistake, I have in my writings called the soul the "transcendental subject" — an expression which Kant also needed by way of exception[*], understanding under that what he calls in numerous places the "intelligible subject", or even the "absolute subject"[†].

This transcendental subject, the soul, does not stand abruptly next to the earthly manifestation of the human; for if the soul possesses the capability for organising, the human is *its* manifestation. Organising and imagination furthermore do not form a dualism within the transcendental subject, but rather just describe two conceptually separable functional movements within itself, but which because of the unity of the subject must always be shown to be actually connected so that the organising shows itself in thought and the thinking in the organising. But because the transcendental subject also forms a unity with his earthly manifestation, the identity of the organising and thinking principle must also be shown within the earthly activity of the spirit, that is, it must show an organisational commitment to it.

Now first of all, as far as the proof that thinking is tied up with an organising, that is to be found in the fields of aesthetics and technology. However, for a theory which misplaces the soul in the unconscious, this task is defined as proving that in the special case of our aesthetic and technological products an organising principle unconscious to us is exposed. If we, for example, see that the formal principle of dividing up of our body, the golden section, also shows itself in Greek temples and Gothic cathedrals — without it having been consciously employed by the builders — then the iden-

---

[*]   Immanuel Kant, Kritik der reinen Vernunft, ed. Karl Kehrbach (Leipzig: Reclam, 1877), 296, 482, 699.

[†]   Immanuel Kant, Prolegomena zu einer jeden künftigen Metaphysik die als Wissenschaft wird auftreten können (Frankfurt & Leipzig, 1794), 134-136 §46.

tity of the organising and thinking elements is thereby proven*. This shows itself still more conspicuously in our technological inventions, with which the unconscious seems to be completely eliminated. They seem to run entirely in the light of consciousness, since in the rule there is a quite purposeful working towards the solution of a specific technical problem in a mathematical treatment. But with the simplest mechanisms, as with the most complicated apparatuses, a spiritual undercurrent is detectable, and that it emanates from the organising element is shown in that the technical apparatuses are only unconscious copies of parts of our body, so-called organ projections, without the inventor having wanted to make a copy†. So, for example, with the camera obscura the eye is in no way being copied with conscious intent, but rather inversely the arrangement of our eyes were first understood when the camera was invented. It is thus more than a mere comparison when you say the lens of the photographer corresponds to the crystal lens, the aperture to the iris, the shutter to the eyelid, the elastic extension to the contractable eyeball, the chemistry of the photographic plate (by virtue of the silver bromide coating) to the light sensitive rhodopsin of the retina. The organs of hearing are understood in the same way when you invoke the piano for explaining, or the nervous apparatus by the telegraph. Even the latest invention, the phonograph, has an organic model in the human brain whose activity in delirium often plays mechanically so that long talks are repeated word for word which the ill person once heard but had forgotten.

Incidentally, the organ projections are very suited for freeing the problem of which beings might live on other stars from the stage of fantasies and giving it a scientific expression with which any monist must above all agree, as paradoxical as

---

* Cf. Adolf Zeising, Neue Lehre von der Proportionen des menschlichen Körpers (Leipzig: Rudolph Weigel, 1854); Franz Xaver Pfeiffer, Der Goldene Schnitt und dessen Erscheinung in Mathematik, Natur und Kunst (Augsburg: M. Huttler, 1885).

† Carl Gustav Carus, Physis: zur Geschichte des leiblichen Lebens (Pforzheim: Flammer, 1860); Ernst Kapp, Grundlinien einer Philosophie der Technik: zur Entstehungsgeschichte der Cultur aus neuen Gesichtspunkten (Brunswick: Westermann, 1877).

it might also appear at first glance. If the identity of the organising and the thinking part of all living beings applies to the inhabitable planets, it would turn out that in all of nature the organic realm and that of technology mutually complete each other. Some of our technical apparatuses have perhaps their organic model on other planets, and some of the organisms of our earth which we have not yet copied technologically are perhaps on other planets parts of the technical array. Beings are conceivable whose eyes are arranged telescopically or microscopically, and the inhabitants of Mars perhaps possess the technological wings which are given to us at present only organically*. If all the planets stand on different steps of development, then the dividing line between the organic and the technological realm is surely drawn for each in a different place whose position also advances with further development. If the organic and the technological realms mutually complete each other, what an abundance of organic life and of life forms unknown to us are then to be thought of! And what an abundance of experiences which we can barely guess at arise in turn from the standpoint of these unknown life forms! It is as if we thought all our current and future apparatuses were equipped with consciousness. How much more than us would, for example, a being know which had the spectroscope in organic form and thereby was sensitive to the chemical qualities of things like our somnambulists are to a certain extent. But also how different from our world would the world appear for such organisations to whom our technological parts were given organically! We can also obtain a practical benefit from this viewpoint. The organ projections contain for us a theory that we do not let accident reign in the realm of inventions, but with purposeful seeking after the solution of technical problems we first look around for organic patterns and shall possibly copy them; for in nature these problems are always solved in the simplest way, because the evolution of nature moves on the line of least resistance. We could already now be flying if we, instead of wasting our time with the search for a steerable balloon, had copied the organic wings.

---

*   [Tr.: note that this was written before the Wright brothers' flight.]

Returning again, thus also showing itself in the activity of the artist, in as much as they are geniuses, thus coming from the unconscious, is the participation of the organising element. Thus with the anthropomorphic and anthropopathic observation of nature by the poet. The poet brings about vivid descriptions of nature only by enlivening and animating the lifeless. The typical characters of a Shakespeare or a Walter Scott are in no way merely conscious imitations, but rather entire actual creations with the participation of the organising soul. Every brilliant series of thoughts has something of an organism in itself, has main ideas and limbs, and it is not mere comparison when we talk of the skeleton of a plot.

The other proof, however, is still to be furnished, that the earthly organising is tied up with a transcendental thinking, in other words that the form of our body is a teleological one, that is, it is bound up with transcendental imagination. Biology, which should furnish this proof, does not show itself to be up to its task; hence we do better to draw on the occult sciences in which the proof will be furnished much more conclusively. To this end we must dedicate a few words to hypnotism and somnambulism.

Hypnotism teaches that organic changes can be brought about through suggestion, that pathological states can be eliminated and those organic processes can be instituted which the doctor considers to be advisable. Those physiological functions which run unconsciously for us, and are beyond our control, e.g. blood circulation, secretions, etc., can be regulated by suggestion. Now it is furthermore clear that the doctor is perhaps incapable as it were of intervening in a foreign organism through words with magical effects; rather the suggestion can only have an effect in that it is accepted by the patient, and this obedience is achieved simply by setting the patient in a hypnotic sleep, thus in a state of psychical dependence. Hence the possibility even of criminal suggestions.

The foreign suggestion is thus only effective because it is transformed unresistingly into an autosuggestion, and only this is the actual agent. The patient thus controls his organic life through the imagination, and with that the primacy of the spirit over the body is proven. Materialism, which on the contrary makes the spirit a mere function of the body, is thus placed on its head, the way you almost always hit the truth when you turn what materialism teaches on its head.

From the entry of organic changes through autosuggestion with the hypnotised patient, the logical possibility now follows first of all that the other normal organic functions are also tied with a transcendental imagining unconscious to us and are regulated by it. This logical possibility, however, is transformed into empirical certainty when we take into consideration the facts of somnambulism. We see, for example, that the somnambulists perform their own diagnosis and prognosis, that thus the organic functions only run the brain unconsciously, but in fact are bound with the transcendental imagination which belongs to the soul. Such abilities, even if they were not given in reality, are a priori probable for a theory of souls which proves the identity of the organising and the thinking elements. In such a theory of souls the medical abilities of the somnambulists do not stand there as isolated facts which you do not know what to do with, but rather they assume their fixed place in a total system of related phenomena. This system would show an inexplicable hole if indeed a transcendental organising were detectable in thinking, but no transcendental thinking in the organising; if thus the medical somnambulists were not to be found in reality. On the contrary, however, the medical somnambulism could not be conceptually incorporated so freely into the new theory of souls if it were not a fact of experience. Anyone who has obtained from the organ projection and from the artistic manner of production the view that the imagining is bound with an organising element will suspect in advance that organic functions are accompanied by transcendental imagination as is shown empirically in somnambulism.

Now the official science has indeed capitulated before the facts of hypnotism — finally after 50 years! — about the facts of somnambulism, however, especially about distant viewing and distant working, it still does not want to know anything. This obstinate denial of facts rests in turn only on the assumption founded on the old theory of souls that our *entire* nature lies illuminated in our self-awareness. There is with this view only room for the normal abilities of the human. If on the contrary the actual core of our nature lies in the unconscious, then very numerous powers and abilities of the soul can be unconscious to us. As soon as you furthermore understand that our earthly person is the manifestation of the transcendental subject, you must also confess that those powers and abilities can also themselves become evident in the earthly person in exceptional cases. For that even an assumption suffices which has been put forward by the natural sciences themselves — the movability of our threshold of perception. Both halves of our nature, the conscious and the unconscious, the earthly person and the transcendental subject, are indeed not divided by an insurmountable barrier, but rather simply by the threshold of perception. We cannot at all claim that those impressions of the outside world of which we are conscious are the only ones which affect us. Rather the natural sciences themselves have proven that we are only conscious of the greatest impressions, those which possess a specific strength of stimulus, whereas an indeterminable wealth of impressions runs below our threshold of perception because of too low a strength of stimulus and remains unconscious to us. What now goes on in the unconscious, that is just the property of the soul, and when this soul receives impressions of which we have no idea, it can on account of them also possess abilities of which we have no idea. But that such abilities pass over to the earthly person, for that the movability of the threshold of perception suffices. But this is a fact. Already in the change from sleeping to waking the threshold shows itself to be relocatable. This individual movability is, however, a necessary prerequisite of its biological movability; without that the entire biological process with its increase in consciousness would be impossible; since this is a fact, however, its logical prerequisite must also be a fact. But whenever the individual movability occurs, the abilities of our unconscious, our soul, must emerge from latency, and it shows itself in somnambulism. It is therefore only a defect in thought when the official sciences hesitate to draw the consequences from the premises that they themselves have put forward.

The transcendental psychology which we first became acquainted with in somnambulism is thus an entirely unavoidable assumption; it follows basically from the mere existence of an organ for physiological psychology; this organ, the brain, is only conceivable as the product of an organising element, and the teleological organising of this brain is only conceivable when this organising is at the same time a thinking.

The new theory of souls with the occult sciences as empirical foundation lies thus in the extended line of the natural sciences and can already be obtained from the current degree of development of the latter. But instead of seeing this, materialists and pantheists still deny the soul, and the adherents of the old theory of souls are still seeking it in the wrong place. It must be confessed, over nothing else has so much illogical stuff been written as over the human soul, both by spiritualists, and still more by materialists, with whose wisdom you are absolutely always reminded of the claim of Montesquieu: "Lorsque Dieu a créé les cervelles, il ne s'est pas obligé de las garantir." [When God created brains, he did not have to guarantee them.] In the end, tired of the dispute, you have to throw in the towel and our modern science which is smitten with the macrocosm does not know where to start with psychology. As Augustine said in his Confessions (Bk. X, Ch. VIII, §15), "There the humans go and admire high mountains and wide expanses of water and mightily rushing streams and the ocean and the course of the stars, but forgetting in addition to admire themselves." But as we have seen, the view into the microcosm is also not entirely closed to us; you need only seek the soul in the right place and emphasise there the deciding facts, those of the occult sciences. In the theory, Aristotle has already worked out this program. It is essential to investigate, he said (in De Anima, Ch. 1), whether the soul "has all its states in common with the body, or whether it is also given something peculiar [...] Thinking seems still for the most part to belong to the soul alone; but when this too is a sort of figurative imagining, or at least cannot happen without such, then thinking too will not be able to happen without the body. Should activities or states of suffering occur which belong to the soul alone, then the soul would be separable from the body; but should nothing of the sort occur, then the soul would also not be separable."

That is just as terse as well said. Since Aristotle now, however, a new science has appeared of which barely a trace can be found in antiquity — linguistics. We know today much more definitely than Aristotle could have known that in fact our abstract thinking is "a sort of figurative imagining", that all our concepts have arisen from original experiences. Hence we can also see no function in thinking which belongs to the soul as such and apart from the body. Concepts are condensed imaginings; imaginings, however, are functions of senses; thus even abstract thinking belongs indirectly to the corporeal. A real soul which were not perhaps only conceivable, but really separable — and thus suggests Aristotle — does not even follow thus from our highest function which we find in the analysis of consciousness. Surely, however, we would obtain it if a thinking without sensory mediation were demonstrable.

Nothing of that is to be found in the conscious life of the mind or spirit; here all thinking is bound up with the senses and the brain. Hence we must in the seeking after the soul just abandon the analysis of consciousness altogether, which Kant has already said, "The general reason why we cannot explain the future continuation of the soul from the observations and experiences of the human disposition is because all these experiences and observations happen *in connection with the body* [...] Therefore these experiences cannot prove what we could be without the body."[*]

Therefore we are relegated to finding the soul in the unconscious. Only in the facts of the occult sciences do we find the unobjectionable proof of the soul. There we find what Aristotle wanted to have in order to pronounce himself in favour of the separability of the soul from the body, namely activities which "belong to the soul alone". The occult phenomena are in the rule tied to states of sensory unconsciousness and come into being through powers and abilities which are latent in normal states and have nothing to do with corporeality. With that physiological psychology is replaced by transcendental psychology. This sets itself the task of transforming the negative concept of the unconscious into a positive one. It teaches namely that we indeed are right to grasp the unconscious as the opposite of the sensory consciousness, but not of the con-

---

[*]   Kant, Vorlesungen über Psychologie: Mit einer Einleitung: Kants mystische Weltanschauung, 85.

sciousness overall; that the so-called unconscious admittedly possesses a consciousness sui generis, an imagining and a thinking which is not mediated by senses and brain, and whereby the brain, when it is involved at all, takes in those transcendental imaginings only receptively. The facts of the occult sciences show that the so-called unconscious possesses consciousness and memory, thus both those elements on which the concept of a personality rests. This transcendental personality, however, is different from the earthly qualitatively, thus the real duality of our nature in Kant's sense must be acknowledged.

Indeed an attempt has been made to resolve this duality into a mere physiological one[*], whereby the dividing line would lie within the life of the brain, not between brain and soul, whereby thus both halves would be affected by death; but this attempt at interpreting the unconscious only physiologically succeeds only so long as you straightaway leave aside the most important phenomena and quite arbitrarily only acknowledge such as find a place in the physiological unconscious. The physiological psychology which, as if by a false switch position, has steered the entire train of our thoughts over the soul onto a false line, will itself never succeeded with a double ego in explaining the likes of distant viewing and distant working from corporeality, hence it denies these facts which do not fit into its system. But those who encounter these facts have also from time immemorial acknowledged their value as evidence for a soul separable from the body. Thus, for example, Deleuze, one of the best connoisseurs of somnambulism, who says, "the phenomena which somnambulism offers us allow us to differentiate two substances, the doubled existence of an inner and an outer human in one and the same individual; they give the best proof of the immortality of the soul and the best answer to the objection which has been made against its immortality; they raise above all doubt the truth already acknowledged by the old wise men and expressed so beautifully by Bonald that the human is an intelligence served by the tools of the senses."[†]

---

[*]   Max Dessoir, Das Doppel-Ich (Leipzig: Ernst Günther, 1890).

Admittedly if you deliberately avoid the way to Damascus, you will also never become a Paul, and if you never see a somnambulist, you can boast for evermore about being a Saul. Anyone, however, who decides to observe somnambulism in its higher phases — in which there is something more to see than hysteria — that great fact in which the doctors put everything that they do not understand — will also soon enough acknowledge the soul. Thus Georget, who in his "Physiologie du système nerveux" reproached somnambulism and lectured materialism, shortly afterwards, however, he attempted himself to treat by mesmerism, and since he acquainted himself with the abilities of the somnambulist, he was immediately converted to the belief in the soul. But he could only give expression to his conviction in his testament in which he said, "I had barely published the 'Physiologie du système nerveux' when new contemplation over an extraordinary phenomenon, somnambulism, did not allow me anymore to doubt the existence present within us and outside us of intelligent principles absolutely different from material existence; we say: soul and God. I have on this point a deep conviction grounded on facts which I consider irrefutable. The statement of mine will first see the light of day when you cannot doubt anymore my sincerity and cannot suspect my views anymore. Should I not be able to publish it myself, then I ask imploringly those persons who are informed of them at the opening of this testament, that is, after my death, to give it every possible publicity."[*]

Everywhere we encounter a researcher who is familiar with the occult sciences, we find also always more or less clearly the same conclusions drawn — that the soul lies in the unconscious, that it is individual, and that we are of a dual nature, a "homme-esprit" [man-spirit] as Saint-Martin put it. Thus already in antiquity with those philosophers who were privy to the mysteries, and so too with the medieval occult-

---

[†]   Joseph Philippe François Deleuze, Praktischer Unterricht uber den tierischen Magnetismus, trans. F.X. Schuhmacher (Stuttgart: Hallberger, 1853), 97.

[*]   Maurice Martin Antonin Macario, Du sommeil, des rêves et du somnambulisme dans l'état de santé et de maladie (Lyon & Paris: Périsse frères, 1857), 148.

ists. "The human [says Paracelsus in de gen. sult.*] has two bodies, the elemental and the sidereal, and both these bodies give a single human. Death parts both bodies from each other in their life." "Thus pay attention that two souls are in the human, the eternal and the natural; that is two lives; one is subject to death, the other withstands death, *thus also hidden in the human is that which the human is*, and nobody sees what is in him, what only becomes obvious through its works."† "In sleep, where the elemental body rests, the sidereal body is in operation, for it has no rest nor sleep; but when the elemental body is dominating and overcoming, then the sidereal sleeps."‡

Only the occult sciences are thus capable of establishing a theory of souls in Aristotle's sense. The soul indeed lies in the unconscious, but in abnormal circumstances in which the corporeal life is weakened, it steps out partly from its concealment. It is therefore a mere appearance that we only lead a material existence during our lifetimes, and only at death would become privy again to the soul's existence. The human as dual nature leads rather both ways of existence *simultaneously*, and this connection, as Augustine already said, is the actual puzzle. "Modus, quo corporibus adhaeret spiritus, comprehendi non potest ab hominibus, et hoc tamen homo est." [The manner in which the spirit clings to the body cannot be comprehended by men, and yet this is a man.] "The man [says Pascal] is the most wonderful creature of nature. He cannot comprehend what the body is, even less what spirit is, and least of all how a spirit can be bound to the body; this is the peak of difficulty; and yet his nature exists in just that." But this difficulty was not felt much so long as, seeking the soul in the analysis of consciousness, it was thought the puzzle of humanity concerned only the binding of organic material with life, feeling and consciousness. The occult sci-

---

*   [Tr.: I have been unable to identify this work more precisely. Cf. Paracelsus, Der Bücher und Schrifften, des Edlen, Hochgelehrten und Bewehrten Philosophi unnd Medici, Philippi Theophrasti Bombast von Hohenheim, Paracelsi genannt, ed. Johannes Huser (Basel: Conrad Waldkirch, 1589), 10:122.]

†   Paracelsus, 10:50.

‡   Paracelsus, 10:187.

38

ences reveal, however, that the puzzle of humanity lies much deeper. It concerns the binding of a transcendental subject with a material body, two quite different and yet contemporaneous existences of whom one runs entirely outside of our sensory consciousness and one is shown by the perception and effects independent of corporeality. Such a connection appears at first glance to want to drive far more towards the dualistic theory of souls, as if the problem only lay in how the organic material came to sensory consciousness; but we escape the dualism and explain that much more puzzling connection in that we make the soul the organising principle of the body. That, however, does not happen arbitrarily, but rather it is proven by the facts of the occult sciences that we are the material representation of a supersensory individual principle. That the soul is animating and organising, however, is in the end confirmed after death; for the lifeless body loses its organisation and dissolves into its component parts.

Materialism thus mixes up once again cause and condition when it wants to explain life and organisation from the material itself. The material is not the cause of our life, but probably the self-evident condition for a material existence. Materialism thus only seemingly solves the puzzle of humanity in that it conjures away the actual problem; the old theory of souls of the spiritualists, however, does not solve it either, and mislays it in a wrong place, seeking the soul in consciousness. A small amount of reflection, however, could have kept us from that; for in the womb we have no consciousness, it first comes to fruition after the birth in the course of years; an entire third of our existence passes by without consciousness, and during our entire life an entire half of our functions, the organic, remain unconscious to us. If we now, however, can *live* without consciousness, then the power preserving us must necessarily be different from consciousness, that is, the soul must lie in the unconscious. We recognise this preserving power in hypnotism, but even more in somnambulism, as a forming and organising power, and indeed bound with a transcendental consciousness which betrays much richer connections to nature than the sensory consciousness has. The higher abilities flowing from that have since time immemorial excited the astonishment of occultists so much that they inferred from this a divine origin for the human soul and its immortality. "We have to seek the distant working magical power [said van Helmont] in the part of us which is the image of God."[*] To the myth that humans were made in God's image, the occultists have given a far deeper sense than usually occurs. When you understand namely this reflective property as being of the earthly human, then Voltaire is right, "Tant pis pour Dieu, si je lui ressemble!" [Too bad for God if I resemble him!] The occultists, however, apply this reflective property to the transcendental subject. Thus van Helmont: "I say that the human is an animal gifted with reason; the true human, however, is no animal, but rather the true image of God."[†]

The occultists also base the proof of immortality on the magical abilities which are not to be explained from the corporeal, thus assuming a bearer separate from the corporeal, a soul. "Our soul possesses [said Agrippa] an all-encompassing sharp eye which is obscured and hindered by the darkness of the body and mortality, but after death, when the soul freed from the body achieves immortality, it arrives at complete cognition. Hence sometimes those near to death and those weakened by age are accorded an unusual beam of light, because then the soul is less shackled by the senses and already as it were freed somewhat from its burden and the place to where they will wander, standing closer, is no longer so subject to the body as previously."[‡]

But these magical abilities of the soul could never become objects of experience if we did not lead both ways of existence, the material and the transcendental, simultaneously. If the transcendental subject were to forfeit its transcendental nature at birth and exchange it with the earthly; if the earthly existence were an interruption and replacement of the transcendental existence which would only be acquired again in death, then there would indeed be a spiritualism, but no somnambulism. With such an assumption we would shut off

---

[*]   Jan Baptist Van Helmont, De magnetica vulnerum curatione (Paris, 1621), § 89.

[†]   Van Helmont, § 83.

[‡]   Carl Kiesewetter, Geschichte des neueren Occultismus. Geheimwissenschaftliche Systeme von Agrippa von Nettesheym bis zu Carl du Prel (Leipzig: Wilhelm Friedrich, 1895), 29.

the path to understanding the occult sciences and the puzzle of humanity, indeed there would be no occult sciences apart from spiritualism. The occult phenomena are perhaps only possible and conceivable under the condition that we lead both ways of existence simultaneously. The assumption is quite inadmissible that we would by the various operations whereby we make ourselves and others ecstatic transform ourselves back into transcendental beings as a result of which then the magical powers of cognition and of the will occur. We cannot assume, for example, that a mesmerist is capable of making us see remotely by gestures. Surely, however, we can assume that he sets us in a state of sensory unconsciousness, and that then the latent *already present* transcendental consciousness *eo ipso* [by that act] steps out of latency. Both these persons of our subject — to converse with Kant — must thus exist simultaneously, otherwise no occultism would be possible at all; and the transcendental consciousness emerges by itself when the sensory is suppressed, the way the stars shine by themselves when the sun has set. The stars do not arrive only now — as the ancients suggested — but rather they were already simultaneously there with the sun by whose elimination they simply became visible.

It rests thus on this simultaneity of both ways of existence that we can encounter the magical powers and abilities already within the earthly existence, both the magic of cognition, the supersensory consciousness, e.g. in the distant viewing of somnambulists, and the magic of the will, the magical effects of the will. This can occur as black, harmful magic, like in sorcery and witchcraft, or as white, beneficial magic; thus in the animal magnetism and in religious mysticism.

The occultists have been clear since time immemorial that the human simultaneously leads both ways of existence, the earthly and the transcendental. Kant, however, found the same truth intuitively, although the relevant empirical facts were not at his disposal. He expressed, as we have seen, in words which I did not perhaps at first read into him, that we already are in our lifetimes unconscious minds/spirits and are connected to other minds/spirits. But you can certainly only understand this view of Kant if you adhere to the other side only lying on the other side of a threshold of perception;

for if it were another place than in the here and now, then both our halves of existence would live spatially apart, the one perhaps in Munich, the other in cloud cuckoo land. But, Kant also did not understand it that way at all. The other side is to him simply the other side of a threshold of perception; he also expressed that in words which cannot be interpreted in any other way: "But if the soul parts from the body, then it will not have the same sensory view of this world; it will not look on the world as it appears, but rather as it is. Accordingly the separation of the soul from the body consists in the *change of the sensory view into the spiritual view; and that is the other world. The other world is accordingly not another place, but rather just another view.*"* When Kant furthermore says: "As little as empirical physics belongs to metaphysics, *just as little does empirical psychology also belong to metaphysics*"† — then with these words he expressly does without finding the proof of the soul in the analysis of consciousness, that is, he says that the soul lies in the unconscious and is only to be proven from the facts of transcendental psychology. I thus find myself in every respect in harmony with Kant, and if my various opponents claim that I misunderstand Kant, then I must assume that they either do not understand German, or that they are lacking in honesty.

"Every human [said Swedenborg] is spirit within."‡ Indeed he goes still further: "Every human is also, while he still lives in his body, with regard to his spirit in the company of spirits although he knows nothing of it."§ With that Swedenborg is saying exactly the same thing as Kant: "It will yet be proven that the human soul even in this life stands in an indissolubly linked community with all non-material natures of the spiritual world, so that it alternately acts in them and receives impressions from them which it is not conscious of as a human, so long as everything is okay."** But later, in his critical period, he said, "Places are only circumstances of bodily

---

* Kant, Vorlesungen über Psychologie: Mit einer Einleitung: Kants mystische Weltanschauung, 92.
† Kant, 5.
‡ Emanuel Swedenborg, Auserlesene Schriften, 1. Auflage (Frankfurt am Main: Christian Hechtel, 1776), 2:200 [Heaven and Hell §453].
§ Swedenborg, 2:188 [§438].

things, not though of spiritual things. Accordingly the soul, because it takes no place, is not to be seen anywhere in the corporeal world. It has no specific place in the corporeal world, but rather it is in the spiritual world; it is in connection with and in a relationship to other spirits."[*]

With these words by Kant and Swedenborg, the condition is clearly described under which mystical phenomena are absolutely possible, that is, under which they can become objects of experience. We can only receive information from a supersensory world if we are ourselves spirits, and indeed already in earthly life, and if we are connected as spirits with other spirits. Both these conditions provide the logical cause for the classification of all mystical phenomena — the one belongs to somnambulism, the other to spiritualism. In somnambulism we get to know our own spirit, our projection into the spirit world; in spiritualism the foreign spirits, the projection of the spirit world. In modern terms Kant's view is thus that we are unconsciously both somnambulist and medium.

A priori that can obviously not be denied; for our sensory consciousness cannot know at all what is given in the unconscious. It thus all comes down to experience whether perhaps these unconscious relationships become conscious to us by way of exception. That can occur, however, when a further condition is added to the simultaneity of the two ways of existence — transcendental insights which we actively obtain as somnambulists, or passively receive as mediums can become conscious to us, that is, pass into sensory consciousness, when the threshold of perception which forms the partition between both persons of our subject is moved. The movability of the threshold of perception is now a biological fact and one of the individual life of the soul, and it proves the real unity of both persons of our subject. The other side as well, as our otherworldly transcendental nature lies only on the other side of the threshold. The movability of the threshold proves furthermore that the phenomena of somnambulism and spiritualism

---

[**]   Kant, "Träume eines Geistersehers, erläutert durch Träume der Metaphysik," 277.

[*]   Kant, Vorlesungen über Psychologie: Mit einer Einleitung: Kants mystische Weltanschauung, 92.

must at least appear in the biological future, that is, with still further movement of the threshold, if they were not already facts of experience today, that is, with the current degree of transposition. Thus today Kant would have found what he had suspected to be empirically confirmed. Hence nothing is so certain as that Kant today would be a spiritualist; for to the extent that a man of his time could be, he was.

Now admittedly when just the word spiritualism is mentioned the modern enlightened become quite nervous. But no cause at all exists for agitation. Rather it only betrays a lack of reflection if you believe you can keep the resistance against spiritualism at all upright. You can deliberately avoid the facts of spiritualism and of course not risk being dragged violently into a sitting. But the defender of spiritualism can break any resistance also on logical grounds, and finally could even have it shown that the natural sciences themselves, without knowing it, have proven the truth of spiritualism. I want to do both here.

Firstly I could point out that in somnambulism we become acquainted with a perceiving and working independent of corporeality, and whose bearer, the transcendental subject, cannot be affected by bodily changes, thus not even by death. But if the bearer is now immortal, then we are faced with spiritualism. If the person in the somnambulist state shows as a spirit, then they are of course also after death, and it just concerns the subordinate question of whether this disembodied spirit can enter into experience. Even this question, however, must be be answered in the affirmative; for in life, in somnambulism, this spirit does not enter into experience by virtue of its corporeality, but rather despite it. If thus this bodily hindrance, which in somnambulism is eliminated only partly, falls away entirely in death, then the manifestations of this spirit must occur in several respects even more easily than in life. It is hence very understandable that you hear, for example, much more about ghosts than about doppelgängers.

Those now are logical grounds by which spiritualism can be proven a priori, but admittedly only under the assumption that the facts of somnambulism are true. Since I cannot, however, force my opponents to study somnambulism, it just remains for me to show that the natural sciences themselves have proven spiritualism.

Our earthly experience depends upon our earthly organisation. If we ourselves only assumed that the senses given to us have a different threshold of perception, then our world view would already have changed thereby. If we assumed that our mere speed of sensory perception were shortened or lengthened, then we would see a whole different world. This has been worked out in detail by one of the thinking naturalists, namely Ernst von Bär, in a treatise that is extremely worth reading*. Furthermore, had the nervous system given to us had a different anatomical progression, so that the tools of the senses which are divided in us were connected by anastomosis, then we would perhaps hear light phenomena or taste tones. Had we in the back of our eye instead of the retina bundles of nerves which were connected with the cochlea in our ear, then we would hear what we see; we would not see the rainbow as a seven-coloured spectrum, but rather hear it as a sevenfold scale. Beings of this sort would perceive a sort of harmony of the spheres where we see the starry sky, and yet their astronomy could be just as exact as our own. Likewise a sort of omnisense could be produced by the comprehensive connection of all sensory tools so that every process of nature would speak to all our senses. With that too our experience, our world view would be changed. But if we assume we would have quite difference senses than those given to us, then our present world would disappear and a quite different one would stand there. In this way inhabitants of the same planet could exist next to one another without having the tiniest inkling of each other. Incidentally our transcendental subject is such an inhabitant of earth, of whom we know nothing. But even in respect to the brain it is a quite self-evident sentence that our experience depends on our organisation. The horse which Moltke rode in the year 1870 had in the same situation as its rider a far lesser experience, and a genius

---

*   Karl Ernst von Baer, "Welche Auffassung der lebenden Natur ist die richtige? und wie ist diese Auffassung auf die Entomologie anzuwenden?," in Reden gehalten in wissenschaftlichen Versammlungen und kleinere Aufsätze vermischten Inhalts, vol. 1, 3 vols. (St. Petersburg: H. Schmitzdorff, 1864), 237–84.

learns more on a stroll than a fool on a journey around the earth.

These sentences are entirely unquestionable, and proven by the natural sciences themselves. It also sheds light, however, on the entire stupidity of materialism. It rests on the experience which only applies to our organisation, it abstracts from it laws which only apply to us, and now believes to have discovered universal rules in it! In fact, however, it has, when it proves these natural laws so exactly, discovered only subjective laws valid for human nature. For a different organisation a different experience applies, and from a different experience different natural laws also follow. A Ludwig Büchner*, if he were to speak before beings of a different organisation about his supposed universal laws, would be simply laughed at.

With every organisation experience changes; materialism concedes that. With experience, however, the laws abstracted from it also change; if the materialist denies that, then you can truly say that he does not understand himself. Every world view which wants to ground itself on mere experience, and which neglects or would like even to forbid philosophical contemplation over this experience must thus be described above all as a childish naivety.

If we now assume beings whose organisation would have no similarity to our own — and whose enormous biological wealth already shows the familiar nature of the little planet which we inhabit! — beings who would be imperceptible to us, and us to them, then changes could arise in the world present for such beings which contradict the laws applying in our world in accordance with our organisation. Since now, however, with the given development of the mutual series of organisations in that and our world — worlds which could even coincide spatially — the ways of perception of the mutual inhabitants could also come into contact, indeed must, it would be very well possible that those changes in that world despite their contradicting the laws applying to us would fall with respect to their effects within our perception, within our

---

*   [Tr.: Friedrich Karl Christian Ludwig Büchner (1824–1899) was a leading proponent of 19th century scientific materialism.]

experience. It would, observed from the standpoint of our laws, be a wonder, but, observed from the standpoint of that world, a process in accordance with the laws of nature. The wonders of the earth, Jean Paul said, are the laws of heaven. Such processes now whose cause lies in that world, but whose effect falls in our world, in our perception, spiritualism offers in abundance. With the spiritualistic phenomena two worlds come into contact whose organisations, thus also there experiences, are different, and in which thus different natural laws apply. Changes in that world, however, could also emanate from its inhabitants themselves. If we think of natures of such coarse materiality as far surpasses iron, then such could travel through granite with their bodies as we pass through the air. If we think of other beings of such an infinitely ethereal rarefaction that they, like even the ether itself, could pass through the pores of granite, then granite would not even be present for such beings. These two types of being would, however, mutually declare each other to be impossible, exactly as Ludwig Büchner denies the fact that ghosts enter through closed doors.

From this standpoint now spiritualism stops being paradoxical. If the materialist thus suggests that the natural sciences will never acknowledge spiritualism because it contradicts our natural laws, then it proceeds from the above that a reflective natural science can already accept it today, and must at least a priori confess its possibility. Everything comes down to the experience which you, however, admittedly to not experience when you have it like those professors who hesitate to come when I invite them to a spiritualist sitting. When materialism suggests that spiritualism must be rejected for all eternity, then it thus does not understand itself; for spiritualism lies in the line of extension of the natural sciences, indeed it is a logical consequence from materialistic premises.

With that we can again turn to the theory of souls which can indeed also be established firmly without spiritualism, but for which spiritualism provides the value of a further confirmation.

The relationship of both persons of our subject is of such a sort that indeed the soul is unconscious to us, more correctly:

unknown to us, but we are not unknown to the soul. That is why we awaken from somnambulism without memory, whereas conversely the transcendental consciousness, as the larger circle, encompasses the smaller circle of the sensory consciousness. We can thus compare the human with an ellipse of which one focal point — the transcendental consciousness — illuminates the entire surface of the ellipse, whereas the other — the sensory consciousness — emits a different light which also only covers half the extent. Or we could compare it with a sphere whose stereometric centre illuminates the cubic content, whereas the light of the sensory consciousness lights up the surface but sends no ray into the interior.

Physiological psychology wants to solve the puzzle of humanity as it were geometrically, and before it lies only the problem of how sensory consciousness and life can be bound to organic material. Now because stereometric problems, however, are not to be solved geometrically, physiological psychology ends with ignoramus [we do not know], indeed ignorabimus [we will not know]. Transcendental psychology by contrast is up to the puzzle of humanity; it solves the stereometric problem stereometrically. Before it lies the much deeper problem — which, however, shows precisely through its deepening the solubility of the human puzzle — of how a transcendental subject can be bound to an earthly body. The answer arises from those facts in which the soul shows itself to be an organising element. We encounter these facts in hypnotism, somnambulism, and spiritualism, but also already in aesthetics and technology. That our transcendental subject is capable of organising teleologically explains the body provided with a brain, in which brain, like in a cephaloscope, the transcendental way of cognition is broken up into a sensory way of cognition. That we have a consciousness at all is an affair of the soul; that this consciousness has an earthly form for the body is an affair of the brain. We for our part have thus no ground for sighing ignorabimus.

The new theory of souls which rests on the facts of transcendental psychology thus shows unmistakable advantages over the old one. The old theory of souls is dualistic, the new one monistic. The old one could only *deduce* the soul from the inadequacy of physiology for explaining the human; the new one by contrast shows the soul *empirically*, demonstrates it directly in its functions. The old theory of souls is like the astronomer who deduces from the irregularity of Uranus's movement the existence of the neighbouring planet Neptune; the new theory of souls is like the other astronomer who discovers Neptune with the telescope. You could say that it demands much more understanding to calculate Neptune than to find it with a telescope. I do not dispute that. But if Leverrier had known the position of Neptune, he would have saved himself his calculation; and if we now for every observation of Neptune wanted to calculate its position first, instead of simply setting up the telescope, then we would indisputably be great fools. But we would be just such fools if, in the attempt to establish a theory of souls, we took no notice of the facts of transcendental psychology in which the proof of the soul lies quite directly, and if we by contrast were to limit ourselves to the psychology of normal life from which the soul can only be indirectly deduced, and which must moreover first make the effort to set itself apart from a materialism which we do not need at all.

With our theological faculties the theory of souls has remained stuck in medieval scholasticism; with the faculty of natural sciences it has become materialistic, and with the philosophical the soul has dissolved pantheistically. A monistic and individualistic solution of the problem of the soul can only be hoped for anymore from transcendental psychology with the occult sciences as an empirical foundation. Modern science still bristles against it, but in this respect it has not only remained behind the medieval occultists, but rather is still at a pre-biblical standpoint; for already in the Bible the difference between my soul and I — ψυχή μου and ἐγω — is distinguished. St Paul said: "For what man knoweth the things of a man, save the spirit of man which is in him?"[*] Even from Cicero we could learn: "Intelligendum est, duobus, quasi a natura nos indutos esse personis" [It must be understood that we are, as if by nature, wearing two masks][†]. But

---

[*]   1 Corinthians 2:11.
[†]   Cicero. *De Officiis*. I. 30.

this doctrine is found clearest of all with Kant, and indeed in his lectures from the critical period. However, when I newly published in 1889 the most important part of these lectures, those over psychology, that book was — apart from a few journalistic voices with the accustomed superficiality and in-comprehension — received with that great silence in which the embarrassment of the opponents betrays itself. They could not forgive me the proof that my philosophical views, obtained on the foundation of the occult sciences, coincided with those of Kant who had proceeded intuitively. They were annoyed with me that I was again drawing light on a book which was carefully not accepted into the complete works, was not placed in the public libraries, and which was out of print in the trade; a book in which Kant not only teaches pre-existence and immortality, but also holds the birth of humans up as the incarnation of a transcendental subject, the other side as the mere other side of the threshold of perception, and in which he — even if he does not describe it with the modern word — teaches that we are all unconsciously somnambulists and mediums.

Such a Kant — who, since his views have now been confirmed empirically, would today be quite indisputably, and as much as Schopenhauer, a spiritist — our science can of course not use and, since one cannot accuse me of a counterfeit, only silence remains. Had I by contrast discovered an old blurb of Kant's and published it with a learned treatise over its un-doubted authenticity, then it would admittedly have been a different case, and I would then have barely escaped the offer of a professorship. To the readers, however, who are inter-ested in the occult sciences, I can only strongly recommend the reading of Kant's lectures. The readers will then say to themselves that you can do without the applause which the *dii minorum gentium* [gods of the lesser peoples] refuse, if you have a Kant on your side. But the occult sciences will un-avoidably now, just because they rely on facts, soon be ac-knowledged, and then at least they will no longer hush up the mystical side of Kantian philosophy anymore, but rather point to him as a forerunner of the current movement; you cannot hinder, however, the adherents of the movement from doing so already today.

If you now distinguish with Kant between both our halves of existence, then you could admittedly be tempted to describe the earthly birth as a fall, perhaps a fall from grace, of our transcendental subject, and the body — as the ancients said — as a prison of the soul. But this view does not express the right relationship, because it does not take into account the simultaneity of both ways of existence. The earthly existence is *added* through birth to the transcendental existence, without harm to the latter, and the appearance of detachment exists only for the earthly human and arises from the limitation of his consciousness to the earthly situation, while the transcendental existence disappears optically for him. So there can be no talk of a prison of the soul; but a comparison between the sensory and transcendental consciousness is permitted, and this turns out admittedly in favour of the latter, although we know it only fragmentally. As far as the soul is incorporated in a body, a higher thing is depicted in a lower thing, and in this respect you can admittedly say: "for a perishable body weighs down the soul, and this earthy tent burdens the thoughtful mind"[*].

If we assume — as the old theory of reincarnation makes out to be possible — a human soul is born again in the body of a lower living creature, then it could show no human abilities, but rather only such as are bounded by make-up and use to their new organs. What would, for example, become of the human mind in a body without hands? Helvetius said that if nature had provided our wrists with horse hooves instead of hands and moveable fingers, then humans would have wandered around in the forests without art, without housing, and without the possibility of defence[†]. It is also not to be denied that the human mind could only have developed by virtue of the *entire* human organisation. Without tools, no civilisation; but the hand is, as Aristotle said, the tool of all tools. A spirit/mind can only manifest to the extent its body allows it and in this respect the transcendental subject cannot show in an earthly body all its abilities. But we are comprehending in this earthly body only half of our nature; our tran-

---

[*]   Book of Wisdom 9:15.
[†]   Claude-Adrien Helvétius, De l'esprit (Paris: Durand, 1758), I. c. 1.

scendental way of existence does not stop at birth, and it forms the other half unknown to us.

You can also, as often happens, call life a dream in so far as the world as idea does not coincide with the world itself. You can with Giordano Bruno call earthly life a death in comparison with the future life, in so far as the transcendental life is a much more intensive one; you can with the same author compare procreation with a drink from the Lethe which makes the prior life forgotten[*†], but all these expressions easily give cause to misunderstandings and have from the standpoint of the simultaneity of both persons of our subject only qualified applicability. The same applies to the words "night side of the soul's life"; for the phenomena of transcendental psychology, although they only become evident like distant lightning, are in several respects to be described as the spiritually freer part of our being.

Let us now look at how the problem of death — without doubt the most important problem for a being whose *essence* is the will to live, who perhaps does not have the will to live, but rather is the will to live — is portrayed from the standpoint of the monistic theory of souls. According to materialistic assumptions, this will must be proportional to the happiness quotient of the individual existence; the happy individual must answer in the affirmative to life, the unhappy in the negative. But that is not correct, the will to live is rather a more or less constant quantity independent of the content of life. Even the poor and miserable fear death. That is only comprehensible if the will to live is not only produced through the content of life, but rather is of a metaphysical nature and precedes the life, if it is thus not the effect of life, but rather the cause. To that extent Schopenhauer was without doubt correct; we are will to life, the will is primary. When he adds that the intellect is secondary, it applies only to sensory cognition, the transcendental way of cognition is just as primary as the will to live, that is, our essence is no blind will, but rather a knowing will; it also does not coincide with

---

*   [Tr.: Lethe = river in Hades whose water made souls forget their earthly lives.]

†   Giordano Bruno, De triplici minimo et mensura, 1591, 33.

the substance of the world, but rather is a transcendental subject, an individual soul. Since that is moreover proven to be an organising element, the earthly birth is thus an act of will of this being. It is the one irrefutable consequence from the pre-existence, hence Kant in following Swedenborg drew the inference that our parents are only our adoptive parents[*].

If we reflect furthermore that distant viewing is a capability of the transcendental subject, then it results still further that not only birth itself, but also those life circumstances the individual is given into are a free-willed act of our being. Even then, if these life circumstances absolutely contradict the wishes of the earthly persons, they must correspond to our transcendental goals, and it is only our own individual providence which has defined our fate. The monistic theory of souls thus achieves what no world view is yet capable of achieving — it places humans on their own two feet. In every other world view in contrast we remain entitled either to grumble about the stupid accident of birth, or about the cause of our existence and fate as always thought to be lying outside of ourselves.

If we now consider the content of human life, the struggle for existence which rages on earth biologically, historically, and socially, the hardship and the suffering which is tied up with human existence for the most part, then it appears at first glance completely incomprehensible as to how humans could ever dare to say the words, "And God saw every thing that he had made, and, behold, it was very good"[†]. The struggle for our existence could only be good in the single case of it being the means to an end, but truly not in itself. Only in the former case would the foundation of the world be morally exonerated. Do we now have a right to this assumption? It seems so; for everywhere in nature, in the astronomical, biological, and historical regions, we see as the result of the struggle for our existence advancement and progress. A world rationality is thus an assumption not at all to be

---

[*]   Kant, Vorlesungen über Psychologie: Mit einer Einleitung: Kants mystische Weltanschauung, 89, 90; Emanuel Swedenborg, Vom Neuen Jerusalem und dessen himmlichen Lehre: Nebst einem Vorbericht vom neuen Himmel und der neuen Erde, 1772, § 148.

[†]   Genesis 1:31.

avoided whether we now think of it as personified or not; whether we think of it as outside the laws of nature, or lying within them itself. Thus as certain as development is, just as certain is world rationality, but also just as certainly it is a superhuman problem to want to define it more exactly.

If you consider by contrast this sorrowful world not as the means to a goal that is unknown, but in any case lying in the line of extension of the advancement up until now, but rather as an end in itself, then you must truly say that to be sure the master commends his work, but not the work its master. Everything will turn out okay — humans have every cause to believe that; it was all good — that can apply to the transcendental world which preceded the process of materialisation; but that all is good, this optimism expressed by the world of the struggle for our existence as a goal in itself would be a dastardly conviction which could only be explained by the blindness or hard-heartedness of its representatives. Anyone who is sympathetic must succumb to pessimism; but this pessimism, the justified world view from the standpoint of the earthly person, turns into transcendental optimism from the standpoint of development if the goal of that lies in the transcendent, not within the material world phase.

What applies to the world, applies to us. If our existence, indeed our fate are our own work whose aim is a metaphysical one, then a transcendental optimism can be justified, and death appears to us then only in its true light. Death would be, for beings whose *essence* is the will to live, an appalling institution if it amounted to annihilation; earthly life, which is almost only earthly unhappiness, would be, for beings whose insurmountable urge is for happiness, a perfidious act of cruelty of the natural facilities if it did not serve a transcendental aim, the welfare of our actual being.

Thus the monistic theory of souls obtains from the suffering as well as death a positive side, and it gives the problem of death such an appearance as a result of which we become determined to use life as preparation for the other side. It thus points us to the right conduct of life, it delivers us a moral principle which materialism and pantheism seek in vain. The mystical world view has been reproached for the belief in the other side taking us to much away from the here and now, and making us incompetent for earthly tasks. This danger exists admittedly, as various outgrowths of the Indian and Christian world view have already shown many times. But this danger lies only in the wrongly understood mystical world view which sees in the world something that is not supposed to be, instead of something supposed to develop. On the other hand, it is entirely unavoidable that the belief in the mere here and now must destine us to a perverse conduct of life, that it must hinder us from preparing for the other side. The belief in the mere here and now makes any moral principle impossible; it makes the earthly person the enemy of the transcendental subject; it is hostile to culture and makes the earthly person the enemy of society.

To that extent the problem of death is also the most important problem for humanity as a whole. The form of its solution defines our conduct of life, thus even the structure of our social relationships. These would in fact not be so distracted if humanity thought more uniformly about death, thus would also more uniformly prepare for the other side. If death is only a desouling of the body, then no reason exists for such a preparation at all, but rather only for that wisdom from hardship which is called resignation. If we merely live on in our works, then it stands poorly for most humans, especially the writers — incidentally the good reputation could then even in the best case have nothing to tempt us, because sooner or later it will be said:

> Soon there'll be nobody anymore to say,
> Who you were and like your image
> Which they carried out withered
> Into a blossoming field.
>
> *Martin Greif.*

On the other hand, if death is only a taking from the body of the soul, then it does not appear anymore to be a natural facility about which you do not know whether to say its absurdity or its gruesomeness is greater. If our existence is not enclosed between birth and death, but rather — according to the view of the old theory of souls — has a continuation admittedly not on the other side of the cradle, but on the other side of the grave, then that would be quite beautiful, but also quite incomprehensible; for a soul which began at the same time as the body cannot be immortal. An eternity cannot have a beginning. Our immortality is only then thinkable when existence also has a prolongation on the other side of the cradle, thus in connection with pre-existence. As an externally given gift and only appearing at the moment of death, immortality can surely be believed but not proven; it will only be able to be proven if we derive it from our current already existing state, thus as founded inwardly in our nature.

The old theory of souls does not achieve that at all, but the monistic surely does. For us immortality is not an external gift, but rather the continuation of something already given, of the transcendental subject. For us death is the taking of the body from the soul, but from a soul which was already there before the body. For the old theory of souls furthermore, death is only a great leap into the darkness, because it has nothing to say about the state after death and at most fantasises about it. For us by contrast, positive clues are at our command with regard to the future state. Our transcendental psychology is the psychology of future life. In the occult sciences we get to know powers and abilities which are not fastened to the bodily organism, hence are also not affected by the dissolution of the body, but rather as a result will emerge to the contrary from the state of being bound. If you can see without material eyes, even though differently, then the loss of the eyes does not signify blindness; if you can think without a brain, even though differently, then the loss of the brain does not signify the annihilation of the thinking being. If powers are present which are not fastened to the organism, then the bearer of these powers must be necessity outlast death, and his way of existence on the other side will then just consist in making use of these powers.

In the old theory of souls the psychology of the other side is of indeterminable quality, and no eye has seen, nor ear heard, how it looks on the other side. In the new theory of souls by contrast, the psychology of the other side has as a positive feature just that which we acknowledge in the transcendental psychology of the here and now. Thus even the problem about the composition of the future life can be solved on the basis of facts. That these facts are still disputed today is relatively unimportant; for in any case the question of the soul has already by the mere claim of its reality risen above the stage of mere speculation and become a question of facts. Pure speculations can be continued for all eternity without decision; questions of facts in contrast cannot remain questionable for long, but rather a decision must naturally always soon be found. We will thus in any case with respect to the problem of death not remain much longer in the current wavering. It will soon be resolved in any case.

That it will be resolved in the sense of immortality is no question for the connoisseur of the occult sciences. Anyone who knows these phenomena will at first see through the inconsistencies of the physiological psychologists who even deny with their tongues that organising principle which has formed just these tongues and set them in motion. But that then that organising power survives its product, the body, is understood in itself on logical grounds and is proven once more by the occult sciences, and indeed in the most eminent sense by spiritualism. The philistine certainly, because he according to Brentano only understands rectangular things and often finds even these too round, becomes quite faint at the mere word "apparition". But is then the human something other than just an apparition, than the incarnation of a transcendental subject, thus the most material of all materialisations and already thereby the most wondrous because it lasts much longer than a spiritualist one? Are then such extraordinary assumptions necessary in order to consider a ghost to be possible? Absolutely not; the only necessary assumption is rather that the soul makes use of its organising power — which, as we have seen, is not merely provable from the occult sciences, but rather from aesthetics and technology — namely at the earthly birth, and that it does not forfeit this power at death. That is of course truly obvious. The craftsman who creates a tool can also create it several times, and if one of these tools is destroyed, then you cannot thereby conclude from it the death of the craftsman!

For the connoisseur of the occult sciences the denial of phenomena is so incomprehensible that he can really only agree with Schopenhauer over what he reproached his opponents with, that they were not sceptical, but rather ignorant.

Perthy estimated the literature of the occult sciences at about 30,000 volumes. Now it is admittedly not to be denied that in that much uncritical material is contained, but also not that this literature becomes constantly more critical. One reads, for example, the "Phantasms of the Living" by Gurney, Myers, and Podmore, or the even more recent "Annales des sciences psychiques". In that you will find enough very critical material which is aimed at the proof of immortality. But anyone who wants to have the decisive proof, that from apparitions, they read Crookes or Aksakof*, or seek out a medium themselves. But the opponents do not look to where they are referred, only in order to be able to claim continually that there is nothing to see there; they close their eyes firmly, and then deny the sun. The number of scholars of the official sciences who were able to decide to investigate the disreputable spiritualism is shamefully small. Often they were also only led by the intention of uncovering the supposed swindle; but yet every time Saul became a Paul. Thus Crookes and Wallace, untouched by that chronic spiritual illness, the a priori judgement, investigated spiritualism and were converted. Thus the professors Zöllner, Fechner, Weber, and Scheibner have carried out spiritualist experiments and likewise been converted. Thus only in recent times, the professors Lombroso, Tamburini, Ascensi, Gigli, and Bigioli dared the thought that nature could perhaps be richer in facts than what scholars know, have held spiritualist sittings, and have at least acknowledged the facts. In the records set down and signed by them from 25th June 1891, Professor Lombroso stated, "I am very ashamed and regret having fought the possibility of the so-called spiritualist facts so stubbornly — I say the facts, for with the theory itself I do not yet agree. But the facts certainly exist, and I boast of being a slave to facts." [Io sono molto vergognato e dolente, di avere combatuto con tanta tenacia la possibilita dei fatti cosi detti spiritici; dico dei fatti, perche alla teoria ancora sono contrario. Ma i fatti esistono ed io dei

---

*   Alexandre Aksakof, Animisme et spiritisme: essai d'un examen critique des phénomènes médiumniques, trans. Berthold Sandow, 3rd ed. (Paris: Librairie des Sciences Psychiques, 1906).

fatti mi vanto di essere schiavo.*] Unfortunately this story of conversion gave the matter only partial advantage because two large errors were made. It was an error that Lombroso's sitting in the dark with the medium who was quickly becoming famous was arranged by lay people, whereby immediately the well-known "exposure" appeared. Sittings in the dark are now without doubt the most substantial; but in a time when what happens in the light of day is denied, it is truly inopportune to want to convert doubters through reports of sittings in the dark. A second error was that Lombroso, having barely become a student, already wanted to be a teacher and appeared with a theory. There is now, however, absolutely no science which you could get your head around in a few hours, and that is the case least of all in the most difficult of all sciences, in spiritualism. You must have a great respect for the open and honest revocation of Lombroso; but if he is already now battling the theory of the spiritualists, then he should consider that this theory comes from people who have the advantage over him of many years of investigation.

In the progress of spiritualism certainly nothing will have been changed by it, and the question of the soul will draw the greatest benefit directly from this part of the occult sciences because it not only proves the existence of the other side, but also, even if only as if through a veil, provides insights into it which can then be tested for their agreement with those insights which we have won from somnambulism.

The disadvantage sticks to the old theory of souls that it in the best case only suffices for the whether of immortality, but leaves the how undefined. The theory of souls must, however, solve both questions at the same time, and it can. If it demonstrates powers in humans which are not associated with the body, then it is just these powers which determine the quality of the future existence; for this future existence is — you must always repeat it — identical with the pre-existence and with our unconscious existence in our lifetimes. Those powers do not, however, in any way develop unhindered in the various ecstatic states, we must thus think of them correspondingly in

---

*   Ernesto Ciolfi, "Gli Ultimi Esperimenti Di Spiritismo," La Tribuna Giudiziaria, July 5, 1891.

an intensified way in order to obtain somewhat clear ideas over the future life. We will be able to receive the best information from the ecstatics themselves while they are in their state. To these clues, however, are now added those which spiritualism offers, and we can then employ the cross comparison to see whether the abilities of the spiritualist agree with those of the somnambulist. Thus it must namely be if our unconscious life in our lifetime should be identical to the future one, if somnambulism contains the partial, and spiritualism the entire removing of the soul from the body.

That the transcendental psychology is in fact that of the future life is proven:

1. by the statements of the ecstatic themselves; and
2. by the analogies between somnambulism and spiritualism.

The somnambulists compare their temporary state to that after death. Thus Auguste K.[*], and the seeress of Prevorst[†]. No difficulty exists either in imagining somnambulism as a permanent state. There are enough examples where it was arrested for weeks and months and whereby the somnambulists, because they also still performed the business of the day displayed a normal appearance. The somnambulists place their state above that of waking; they consider it to be the more real and speak with a low opinion of their earthly person. Muratori reports about a girl who after a violent fever lay their apparently dead so that the funeral was already being thought of, until she let out a sigh, at which they brought her around again. But she then burst out wailing that they had torn her away from a state of inexpressible rest and bliss. None of her friends among the living could equal what she had experienced in the least. She had heard the laments of

---

[*]   Johann Karl Bähr, Mittheilungen aus dem magnetischen Schlafleben der Somnambüle Auguste K. in Dresden (Dresden: Arnold, 1843).

[†]   Justinus Andreas Christian Kerner, Die Seherin von Prevorst: Eröffnungen über das innere Leben des Menschen und über das Hereinragen einer Geisterwelt in die unsere, 2nd ed., 2 vols. (Stuttgart & Tübingen: Cotta, 1832); Justinus Andreas Christian Kerner, The Seeress of Prevorst; Being Revelations Concerning the Inner-Life of Man, and the Inter-Diffusion of a World of Spirits in the One We Inhabit, trans. Catherine Crowe (London: J.C. Moore, 1845).

her parents and the discussions regarding the funeral, but her rest had not been disturbed by that — she was not thinking anymore about the preservation of her life*. Often the somnambulists express sadness over the imminent awakening. "How am I not supposed to be sad [said one], since I must again put on the dress, the heavy body."† Some do not want to hear their auto-diagnosis because they place no value on their health; death does not frighten them, they know that they will be happy when they leave their body‡.

The ecstatic state demonstrates even over the corporeal a double advantage, the suppression of the bodily troubles and obstacles, and the intellectual elevation. Sensory cognition has its limits; it only lets us recognise the things according to their appearances. The somnambulists by contrast are affected by the inner substance of the thing; they experience impressions from inanimate things which on awakening they are not at all conscious of, or only as idiosyncrasies. Plants and medicines, even homeopathic, are examined by them with respect to their conduciveness or harmfulness for the organism. The vague sympathies and antipathies by which we are led in dealings with humans are more pronounced and clearer with the somnambulists; it is the inner moral substance of humans by which they are affected.

The reading of thoughts is shown by them more or less perfectly, which therefore, enhanced after the removal from the body, arises as the language of spirits. Likewise we can apply psychometry to the future life, that strange property of sensitive persons who even awake receive from inanimate objects vivid pictures from their past. The same applies to distant viewing and distant working. Telepathy and telekinesis of every sort, which when awake occur by way of exception, will

---

* Lodovico Antonio Muratori, Über die Einbildungskraft des Menschen (Leipzig: Weygand, 1785), 2:81 ff.

† Ernst Daniel August Bartels, Grundzüge einer Physiologie und Physik des animalischen Magnetismus (Frankfurt am Main: Varrentrapp und Sohn, 1812), 182.

‡ Aubin Gauthier, Traité pratique du magnétisme et du somnambulisme ou Résumé de tous les principes et procédés du magnétisme (Paris: Germer Baillière, 1845), 612.

be enhanced in the body-free state above the somnambulist's level.

Without assuming an intellectual homogeneity of all transcendental subjects — which certainly does not exist and also not in moral respects — we will though claim intuition, which in the productions of genius steps in place of reflection, as a transcendental ability and as the form of thinking on the other side. We must also consider the organising ability of the soul to be elevated for us in the future, and will also have to assume an object of that, a somehow created body of the soul which thus in death stops wearing only the coarse material body. Of a purely spiritual state on the other side, of a thinking as substance instead of mere attribute, we cannot form any concept; we will thus consider the future state to be not completely without body. "It is haughtiness [said Baader] to want to be without body."[*] Now we indeed see in waking life the physiological functions of consciousness and arbitrary freewill lost in reverie; but in somnambulism they appear partially accompanied by transcendental consciousness, and in hypnotism partially subjugated to arbitrary freewill in that autosuggestion can call forth organic changes, a discovery which Kant made before Braid[†]. We will thus — always assuming the elevation — consider the future body free of the defects of the earthly one and we will have to acknowledge the psychic method of curing, which with us is only barely in its first stages, as an ability of the future existence.

We encounter the body of the future life, the astral body, already within earthly experience and call it then a doppelgänger. This phenomenon removes the dispute over the organising principle from all physiological and biological objections. Furthermore we encounter the same organising power emanating from the dead, in the spiritualist materialisations, and finally in the earthly birth itself, the most re-

---

[*]   Franz Xaver von Baader, Franz von Baader's Sämmtliche Werke, ed. Franz Hoffmann (Leipzig: H. Bethmann, 1851), 2:15.

[†]   Immanuel Kant, Von der Macht des Gemüths durch den bloßen Vorsatz seiner krankhaften Gefühle Meister zu seyn: Ein Schreiben an Herrn Hofrath und Professor Hufeland. über dessen Buch die Kunst das menschliche Leben zu verlängern (Königsberg & Jena, 1798).

markable materialisation. Our own birth is thus a spiritualist fact, and yet we deny spiritualism!

The astral body has frequently also been called the etheric body, and perhaps we are in fact right to call it thus in a quite essential natural science sense. If the material of the doppelgänger and the materialisation were condensed ether, then the latter and ghosts would even possess those abilities which result from the physical nature of the ether — the quickness in space, the penetration of material, the annulment of gravity. Distant viewing and distant working could thus directly contain a natural sciences' explanation. With spiritualist sittings we encounter phenomena from which are to be concluded an etheric nature of the being manifesting itself and the use of movements in the ether for its expression; but also with the distant working of the somnambulists, especially when material changes come about as a result, etheric movement probably cannot be ignored.

There exist thus analogies between the abilities of the somnambulists and the disembodied, and this is to be concluded from the essential identity and only slight difference between the two manners of existence. These analogies stretch to the material way of working and to intellectual abilities. We encounter the reading of thoughts and the distant viewing in time and space in both areas, somnambulism and spiritualism. And as many cases of somnambulist distant working are probably not explainable as etheric distant working, but rather only by the intervention of the doppelgänger, even if it is also not condensed to the level of visibility, so too with many spiritualist processes a corporeal, even if invisible form of the manifesting power is not easily dismissed, e.g. with direct writing. The way, however, the doppelgänger can achieve a degree of denseness which makes it visible, thus also materialisation which then also could, as is well-known, be photographed and checked for weight the way the pulse and heartbeat can be checked.

To now only briefly adduce further analogies between somnambulism and spiritualism, so-called ghost workings can emanate from both the living and the dead; through mediums the dead can manifest, but so too can the living — who simultaneously lie in a deep sleep — manifest; medical suggestions emanate from somnambulists, just as they do from mediums. Indeed somnambulism is absolutely only a special case of mediumship, they are to each other as autosuggestion and foreign suggestion. The somnambulist is under the influence of his own spirit, the medium under that of a foreign spirit.

All these analogies between somnambulism and spiritualism compel us to reach the conclusion that after death we will be just that which we already were in an unconscious way in life. We are already during life spirits/minds, and the state after death is somnambulism of an elevated sort become permanent and normal.

In such a way the monistic theory of souls, built up on the facts of the occult sciences, thus resolves the whether of immortality together with the how. The more we research this area, the clearer we recognise that death does not signify the annihilation of individuality, nor its dissolution into the world substance, but rather that we continue with elevated individuality, that thus the so-called dead are much more alive than we are. In comparison with the transcendental reality of future existence, Giordano Bruno described — even because he was familiar with the occult sciences — earthly life as a curtailment of individuality: "What we call dying is the birth to a new life and often the current one would probably be called death in comparison with that future life."[*]

The Pythagoreans called death a birthday — γενεσία — of the spirit. In the martyrologies the day of death is called *dies natalis* [day of birth] and Angelus Silesius called death "the best of all things". As given from experience we know only the approximate states of the future state of the somnambulists and, by nature identical, the state of the disembodied so far as they can dive back into the earthly element, which is not possible without losses in ghostliness. Nevertheless from the spiritualist phenomena death also is acknowledged as an increase in individuality, and since as a result the current state betrays itself in a certain sense as a corporeal one, death can be seen as an essentialisation of our entire being, both the consciousness and the corporeality.

———————————

[*]   Bruno, De triplici minimo et mensura.

64

From the resistance which the theory of immortality encounters, you would think it would be utterly unthinkable and only an object of faith. When we dismantle its component parts, however, two questions arise which must both be answered in the affirmative:

1. Can a living being persist amidst a change of form? That is undeniable and is even demonstrated within earthly existence in the well-known development of the butterfly from the caterpillar.
2. Can a living being lose its form of consciousness and persist with an up-to-then latent consciousness? Even that is not to be denied. In the alternation of waking and sleeping we have the change of consciousness and that between animal and vital functions. The dualism of consciousness shows itself even more markedly in hypnotism and somnambulism.

Immortality is thus physiologically and psychologically possible. To that can also be added its logical certainty from the recognition that we are the product of an organising power, and its empirical certainty which spiritualism delivers. But anyone who denies this still has a few things to learn.

Admittedly the old theory of souls was itself to blame that it lost its adherents more and more. So, as it was portrayed, it could not hold out against the advancing sciences. The solution to the problem was wrong because already the question had been placed incorrectly. Namely if you ask, 'where is the other side?', then the doubter could declare the question itself to be superfluous and say modern astronomy has erased the heavens. If you ask what becomes of us after death, then the enlightened could interject that it is absolutely unthinkable as to how a mortal creature is supposed to become immortal at a given moment. If you ask how we arrive on the other side, then a somehow satisfactory answer cannot be given. In short if you regard immortality to be the *acquisition* of a *new existence* and *transportation* to a new place, it cannot be proven; but surely it is provable as the continuation in the same place of a state already given unconsciously. That we *become* spirits in death can surely be spoken, but not thought; but it is surely thinkable and provable through somnambulism that we now already *are* spirits, and that this half of our nature is not impacted by death. The other side is not another place to where we would be transported in an incomprehensible way after death in order to continue living there under quite new conditions of life; it is not spatially separate from the here and now, but rather a mere other side of consciousness.

The other side is the here and now seen differently. But anyone now who wants to see in such an other side a poor replacement for the religious heaven might first consider that the quality of a place does not distinguish whether it is a heaven or a hell, but rather the quality and the relationship of our organisation to the place. The here and now and the other side, although they objectively coincide, can be distinguished as poles apart for the respective residents, indeed perhaps having not the least similarity to one another. The transition from the here and now mode of cognition to that of the other side alone already amounts factually to a transportation into another world, because no similarity exists between the impressions which beings in the here and now and those on the other side draw from the same world. But even the mode of working, thus the entire way of existence of the two-sided resident is entirely different. Even if only that malady which is a given with our coarsely material corporeality were suddenly expunged from our earthly existence, we would seem to be in heaven. At a minimum we are certain of this future heaven, even if no transportation to another place occurs. When we consider moreover that our earthly senses are limits far more than organs of cognition, a considerable increase in cognition must occur with the putting aside of these limits, the way somnambulism already makes us acknowledge that the being on the other side stands in an expanded and much freer relationship to nature than we do, which is increased still more by the manner of local movement befitting the etheric being. In short this earth of ours, already described so often as a valley of despair and place of penitence, could be a place of blissfulness for beings of another way of existence.

Now as two beings can stand in such different relationships to one and the same world that they know nothing of each other and their respective worlds, so too can one and the same being stand simultaneously in two relationships to the world whose difference can be so considerable that one half of the being is unconscious of the other. And that is just the case with the earthly human who already lives unconsciously on the other side and, since death only impacts the half of the being in the here and now, also remains in it.

As long as you misplace the soul in consciousness, which is indisputably physically conditioned, you cannot prove its immortality, and death must appear as that and merely as that which it is admittedly to the one side, a mere robbery, a removal of the soul from the body. But when you acknowledge that the soul is on the other side of consciousness, that we already stand now on the other side, that our sensory consciousness is a limitation of cognition, on the other side of which the supersensory world and in it our supersensory nature lie, then death also obtains a positive side, it then becomes the disembodiment of the soul.

As you see, the disputed issue of immortality did not come to a resolution simply because it revolved around a false object — around the earthly human, around the object of our sensory consciousness. As a result, materialism had to remain the victor. When in contrast immortality is reduced to the transcendental subject, then materialism must lose; for the acknowledgement of this subject too by that side is only a question of time because facts cannot be denied for all eternity. The old theory of souls of the religions has ignored the transcendental subject almost as much as materialism has, and yet it could have even quoted the Bible for it. There namely the creation of man occurs twice. First it states: "So God created man in his own image, in the image of God created he him"*. Then again against expectation it states: "And the Lord God formed man of the dust of the ground, and breathed into his nostrils the breath of life; and man became a living soul"†. You can easily relate that firstly to the beginning of the transcendental existence and then to the earthly existence.

Hypnotism and somnambulism prove that in our unconscious lie powers and abilities of whose use, indeed existence, our sensory consciousness knows nothing because our con-

---

* Genesis 1:27.
† Genesis 2:7.

sciousness is a corporeal one, but those powers do not adhere to the body. When the somnambulist awakes, i.e. comes to bodily consciousness, he is without memory, and therein it is shown that his consciousness was for a moment not bodily. By that it is proven that our self-awareness does not encompass our entire being. Spiritualism shows furthermore that those transcendental powers and abilities of the unconscious are the powers of the future world that is to be expected ahead of us. They are unconscious to us; that cannot, however, possibly be understood as if these forces existed only in the state of mere tension and were non-functioning. They must rather be integrated in an entire system of powers directly like the powers of our earthly person of which we are conscious are integrated into the visible world. That system of powers now to which we unconsciously belong is the realm of the spirits. In this spirit realm we will obviously consciously find ourselves after death because we are already in it now; we will be blessed with the powers of the future world because we already possess them now. The other side is thus not another place, but rather only another side of consciousness; and because our consciousness is made up of the impressions whose level of stimulus is large enough to be felt, you can also say the other side is a mere other side of the threshold of perception.

Only if the human lives simultaneously in the here and now and on the other side is it comprehensible that those powers, by virtue of which we are already now unconsciously spirits, are by way of exception raised over the threshold of perception and enter into experience like, for example, the distant viewing and distant working of somnambulists; only thus is it furthermore comprehensible that those powers appear by nature to be identical with those with which we are acquainted in spiritualism as the powers of the disembodied souls. From that the lesson follows for the spiritualists that they only half understand humans when they — which unfortunately is the case most of the time — do not study somnambulism; and for the materialists the lesson follows from it that, because they study neither spiritualism nor somnambulism, they do not understand humans at all.

All in all it can be said that the solution to the puzzle of humanity by materialism is quite hopeless, that of transcendental psychology much more hopeful. In order to compensate us for this hopelessness, materialism accentuates the life of the species. Nature is not do with the individual, rather it is to do with the species. In the constant progress humanity shall head towards a state which can be thought to finally rise to a golden age. The task of the individual is to play a role in this history of the development of the human race as a helping link.

But this consolation unfortunately does not hold up for long; for apart from that even species die, it is absolutely arbitrary to remain standing on the biological point of view. As a naturalist the materialist must assume the higher, astronomical standpoint — a point in time will occur when the earth will in the end be uninhabitable through the downwards movement of the isotherms from the poles to the equator, but later the earth will disintegrate into a meteorite shower and plunge into the sun. If humanity itself may reach a golden age, it will be missing a legacy anyway. What can absolutely once have a definite end is in any case pointless. Materialistically considered the death of the individual makes the previous life just as pointless as the previous cultural history becomes pointless through the dying out of humanity. You cannot place any goal in any point of the development if you cannot place an end goal at the endpoint.

Indeed, astronomically considered, the game commences ever again anew in that the solar system dissolves into a cosmic cloud and solar systems arise again from this. But the result of the biological and historical process is always lost forever. A pointlessness does not become sensible by its being eternally renewed. It thus lacks all reason for being enthusiastic for the history of the species whose reality moreover does not go beyond that of the individuals. An artist who destroys his work again and again need not be gazed at in wonder, but rather belongs in the madhouse, and indeed all the more, the more his works are those of genius. It is thus a mere cliché when materialism seeks to enthuse us for the magnificence of nature; according to its own premises it must describe them rather as a material absurdity.

It is quite different from our standpoint. The single fact of immortality, introduced into the formula of the world, transforms the world from an absurdity into a magnificently arranged organisation. Firstly what applies to the whole world namely applies to us. As we are the materialisation of a supersensory being, so is the entire visible world the materialisation of a supersensory world, and indeed the world also leads, like ourselves, both ways of existence simultaneously. We thus do not encounter with our judgement of the visible world the entire world, and if this judgement itself were to make us pessimists, then it could be expressed only with the reservation that the one-sidedness of our standpoint must presumably result in a one-sided judgement, which could essentially turn out differently if an overview across both halves of the world were granted to us.

Now, however, the visible world, even considered one-sidedly, in no way forces a confession of pessimism from us. Indeed the eternal cycle of the worlds exists, and in all of nature every biological and historical process sooner or later has an end; but only for the materialist is it an eternally repeating absurdity, only the pessimistic pantheist must recognise in it at least a passing absurdity ending with the suicide of God. But for us, in that we only again introduce immortality into this cycle of the worlds, the apparent end in itself of nature becomes a mere means to the goal. The cycle only concerns the external locale of nature and it is not an end in itself, but rather arranged with a view to producing life in an eternal variety; but this eternally repeating breaking off of biological developments again only concerns the material half of life; the accent, however, lies on the supersensory half of life of single individuals, and only nature is only concerned with this, with the constant raising of forms and their consciousness within the visible world, and for that reason, that the reward for their effort is not lost to the single individuals of the invisible world. But that is also now the case. The product of our life remains preserved for us. It only vanishes optically for us while its expression is handed over to the unconscious. When we are acquiring a mechanical skill, we begin with consciously slow and awkward movements which gradually transform into unconsciously quick and skilled movements; likewise the conscious thoughts condense into unconscious talents, the moral actions thicken into moral tendencies, while the abstinence from immoral actions draws the atrophy of immoral tendencies after itself. We thus carry the legacy of our efforts and of the result of our suffering within ourselves. We even bequeath the tendencies in two directions; to ourselves in so far as we belong to the invisible world, i.e. to the transcendental subject; and to our descendants in the visible world, to whom our tendencies are transferred so that in the successive generations the individuals find an ever more suitable medium for further developing in the sense of culture, which then again redounds to the credit of their transcendental nature, and reduces cultural history to a secondary goal.

Life thus has an individual goal, but it is transcendental. The goal is there because the earth is there. The cultural history of humanity is also functional, but in the last instance again only for the transcendental nature of the individuals. The goal moreover does not lie perhaps merely in the biological and historical endpoint of earthly development, but rather it is fulfilled along the entire line of the process. Might the historical waves of culture also smooth out again and again and raise new waves spatially transposed; might the planets also perish and the solar system vanish, the result of the development though is not lost; the transcendental goal has fulfilled itself from beginning to end, and with the end has also reached the end goal. The eternal change in the visible world has a lasting result for the invisible. Even in the invisible world and for our invisible nature development thus takes place because the results of our visible life are sucked up.

If now, however, the work of our life is bequeathed in two directions, to the transcendental subject and to our earthly descendents, then it can be asked whether the earthly and transcendental development shall only ever act as means to the goal, or whether they are perhaps destined to be united. On the one hand namely our unconscious and that which is awarded to the unconscious by the acquisitions of life are conscious possessions of our soul. On the other hand this unconscious is the source from which the biological process draws while the abilities of the organising soul acquired in the biological enhancement of the forms is preserved and brings forth shining in the biological process ever higher forms. The unconscious is finally also the source of the historical process in that the intellectual and moral tendencies remain preserved and elevate the cultural history. The end goal of this process would thus be that the property of the soul would overflow ever more into its earthly form of appearance and would be itself on the way to reincarnation; that thus the earth finally would bring forth a creature in which the property of the transcendental subject would be united without residue with the property of its earthly form of appearance and all the unconscious would be annexed by the consciousness. Such a being would therefore unite in itself our two natures which today are still separated by the threshold of perception.

That our transcendental powers are unconscious to us is a clear indication that they have nothing to do with corporeality — for our consciousness encompasses only corporeality — and that it is not impacted by death, for death also encompasses only corporeality. That hypothetical future being now, who will perhaps appear on earth and would be in normal conscious possession of our at present still transcendental abilities, would no longer need to pass through birth and death — it would have overcome death in that the soul as organising principle would be united with the physical, and it would no longer stand next to it as its mere product. Only we must not thereby think of the physicality of the current human, but rather of that lifeform up to which the biological process will then have risen. In such a being the bodily would be united with the spiritual because the bodily has risen ever more into the spiritual, and the spiritual has overflowed ever more into the bodily. The simultaneity of the two ways of existence would produce a fusion of the same place. The idea of the transfigured physicality, that is, the uniting of the predominately material with the predominately spiritual existence is an idea of Schelling and disregarding the already current simultaneity he speaks of a succession of *three* states at the end (of the separate edition) of the discussion "Clara"* and in his "Philosophie der Offenbarung"†; but he expects this union, which he equates to the Christian doctrine of the "resurrection of the flesh", from a "crisis" whereas it has in fact prepared itself since the appearance of life through the just as slow as constant shifting of the threshold of perception, whereby the transcendental content of life is just impressed on the earthly.

There are problems which show their depth in that by their solution light radiates out far beyond their own boundaries. Even when we leave it open whether both our forms of existence are called to a former fusion, the problem of immortality alone already in the solution presented here makes the sense of human existence appear in a quite different light than previously. In the solution of the puzzle of humanity we are thus moved closer to that of the puzzle of the world, and if the materialistic as well as pantheistic solutions can only put us in a mood which wavers between embittered despair and mocking gallows humour, then the deepening of the problem, namely the insight that the roots of our individuality lie on the other side of the threshold of perception, in the unconscious and not in the consciousness, results in a view of life which in accordance with we like to take on ourselves the earthly tasks, and from earthly sorrows look on a consoling perspective. Materialism and pantheism can only have a paralysing effect on the individual and as a result on cultural history.

Through the deepening of the puzzle of humanity we are, however, involuntarily drawn into the solution of the puzzle of the world, and now no longer need to declare ourselves in favour of the irrationality of being. If we ourselves are determined on increasing knowledge and morals, then, because we are connected as a very fundamental link in nature, the world itself must be an intellectual and moral problem. As furthermore we are only the materialisation of a supersensory

---

*   Friedrich Wilhelm Joseph Schelling, Clara, oder, Zusammenhang der Natur mit der Geisterwelt: ein Gespräch (Stuttgart: Cotta, 1862), 175–86.

†   Friedrich Wilhelm Joseph Schelling, Friedrich Wilhelm Joseph von Schellings sämmtliche Werke, ed. Karl Friedrich August Schelling (Stuttgart & Augsburg: J.G. Cotta, 1856), 214–18.

being, so too is all of nature the materialisation of a super-sensory world. That the material world would have arisen from nothing, you can anyway surely say out loud, but not think with your brain; but it can surely be thought that by virtue of an unfathomable fate — we might call it fall from grace or the like — the supersensory world or a part of it could have been seized by materialisation, like the individual person at birth. It can also be said that this materialisation could be annulled again like our own material existence so that the eternity of the world would no longer be understood in the materialistic sense as the eternity of the material world. The simultaneity of both our ways of existence would also be set in parallel with the simultaneity of the sensory and super-sensory world. The materiality is thus a phase of development for the individual and for the world.

Materialism and pantheism are very well conscious of their own hopelessness in contrast to the consolation of the mystical world view; but they meet this objection with the words that consolation is absolutely not a necessary feature of the truth. That it is not either, but yet a possible one! The concept "hopeless truth" is not a *contradictio in adjecto* [contradiction in terms]. Consoling world views can also come into being through the wish becoming father of the thought, as with most religions. But the materialists and pessimistic pantheists, in that they wanted to avoid this error, have fallen into the opposite error.

Dum stulti vitant vitia, in contraria currunt [When fools avoid vices, they run to the opposite].

Through habituation to their way of thinking the prejudice developed in them of seeing the hopelessness of the truth as a necessary feature of the truth, and every world view which corresponds to some emotional need seems to them to be already suspect in advance. The popularisers of natural sciences' world view seemingly wallow in the elegiac mood when they consider the earthly life with its painful struggle and the grave mound at the endpoint, when they resolve planets and entire fixed star systems, and they also thereby obtain by easy purchase the respect of souls attuned to sublime poetry.

But to that it is to be countered that the concept "hopeless truth" also does not contain any *contradictio in adjecto*. The

74

mystical world view would then only be faulted if its founders had already been peeking with their thought operations furtively at the consolation and steering their reason. But that is not the case. The mystical world view rests on the facts of somnambulism and spiritualism, and draws from them the unavoidable logical conclusions which absolutely do not need to be linked by necessity with partiality for the comfort of the conclusions. The critic must never criticise the *result* of research, but only the *path* by which it was reached, and likewise the researcher has only to look at the path on which he travels without worrying about where he is going.

The mystical world view comes into being now in a scientific way by logical conclusions from given facts. During his work the researcher seeks the truth and nothing else, and the question of whether it is consoling appear as illogical to him as the question to a mathematician of whether a triangle is green or blue. But this cool objectivity is only necessary during the work in which the mind should be kept free from the blandishments of emotion. But if the emotions declare at the conclusion approval with the results, then that cannot harm the value of the work. Were the mind of the critic to raise an objection for the sake of this result, then he would on his part no longer be objective.

The truth must be transparent like ice; but it need not be ice-cold; and if it is not, the researcher remains free to rejoice over it, as the meteorologist may also as someone out on a walk enjoy a beautiful summer's day he has forecast; it would be silly to desire of him that he may only be permitted to bear his coolness of mind through the forest. If my critics say my world view corresponds to some emotional needs, then they are right, but what can I do about it? If they by contrast say it is predicated on them, I will at most conclude from it that they cannot do me any harm with scientific criticism, with criticism of the path, and are therefore taking up the criticism of the result.

If the facts of hypnotism, somnambulism, and spiritualism are correct and the consequences drawn from them above reproach, then the correctness of the world view produced from them must be admitted for as long until perhaps a different result is produced by the introduction of new facts of experience into the world calculation.

Now hypnotism is acknowledged already, and if individual professors, like Dubois-Reymond and Meynert oppose with their theories the facts which they have not studied at all, then that is just like running head first into a wall, which never turns out to your advantage. Somnambulism is also acknowledged as a phase of hypnotism, and as a result in the near future all those facts will be "discovered" by the professors which were already common knowledge one hundred years ago. I have already explained often enough how fluid in the end the boundary between somnambulism and spiritualism is that I do not have to repeat it here; and if nonetheless Dr Moll in Berlin recently explained the knocking sound of mediums by the banging together of the ribs, then he may be certain of the Homeric laughter of posterity.

The recognition of the entire transcendental psychology is accordingly only a question of a short time, and if there are also modern textbooks of psychology in which somnambulism is not granted the most unassuming space, then it must just be said straightaway that such books, as thick as they might be, are already obsolete on the day of their appearance. What Lichtenberg said applies to "specialists" of this sort: "I have already many times remarked that the people of a profession often do not know the best."

The physiological psychology will more and more demand its recognition as an important branch of knowledge, but it is quite lacking in its ability to solve the puzzle of humanity. Only transcendental psychology can do that. You cannot belittle the latter by referring to its frequent connection with pathological conditions; it is rather a confusion of cause and condition if you conclude from it that the mystical abilities are in themselves pathological. You also cannot belittle it by declaring that the normal psychic abilities are the highest. That they are with respect to practical usability for life, and, as Kant already said, "the cognition of the other world can only be obtained here by forfeiting something from that understanding which you need for the *present* world.".* But nevertheless the transcendental abilities have the greater theoretical significance for the explanation of the human; for they prove that he is not equipped merely for this existence. This proof is harder to carry out from the normal psyche, and only as a result could materialism assert itself so stubbornly; it breaks up though if even only a single case of distant viewing is proven, the way thousands of them have been proven. Of the abilities of the embryo in the womb, the as it were highest are those which are the most important for its embryonic existence; but of much greater philosophical significance are those rudiments which have no significance for that phase of existence, but which are acknowledged as preparing it for entrance into our world of light. Its organs of movement and instruments of sense are for the moment pointless, but we recognise its high calling directly from them.

If we now summarise in brief the grounds which show the significance of transcendental psychology for the puzzle of humanity:

1. Pope said that the actual study of humans is the human. It is a subjective need that we at first want to get some clarity over ourselves; since we, however, indisputably occupy the first rank on earth, we are also objectively the most interesting object of investigation.

2. The efforts to explain the world, and us from it, have up to now turned out so unsatisfactorily that the attempt may be worthwhile to decide the significance of the world from the puzzle of humanity. This way *must* in fact be adopted; the human as highest fact of nature must first be defined correctly if nature itself shall be evaluated correctly. A writer and artist must be judged according to their best works; a Homer not from those places at which he slept according to the remark of Horace: *quandoque dormitat Homerus* [sometimes Homer sleeps]. Only when we know what the human is can we express conclusively what the world is. Since we are structured for consciousness and morality and are created in harmony with nature, nature is also an intellectual and moral problem.

---

*   Kant, "Träume eines Geistersehers, erläutert durch Träume der Metaphysik," 291.

World and human can certainly be kept apart conceptually, but belong together. The entire puzzle of humanity appears in various lights according to whether we comprehend the human materialistically as a merely physical problem, or spiritually as a metaphysical problem.

3. The highest definition of the human arises from transcendental psychology which thus also confers a higher standing on all of nature. The following simile from the area of astronomy will clarify that.

The first who scientifically observed a shooting star will have without doubt adjudged at first sight that from some cause in the atmosphere luminous points arise, move forth with great speed and then extinguish. What eyesight teaches is thereby correctly described, but the nature of the shooting star is not yet recognised with that. It is only understood as a phenomenon belonging to cosmic physics — the shooting star on its tour about the sun arrives occasionally in the earth's atmosphere; through that its spatial movement is hindered and transforms according to physical laws into molecular movement, i.e. heat. The shooting star turns glowing hot and that section of its path which lies within the atmosphere is illuminated; it extinguishes again, however, outside the atmosphere where air resistance is not present; it vanishes optically, but in fact continues its tour. The existence of the shooting star is hence not limited to the illuminated section of its path, but rather extends before and after.

Anyone now who commences the human with the birth, who has the human annihilated by death, is like an astronomer who explains the shooting star as a mere atmospheric phenomenon from the illuminated section of its path. If we only consider the earthly section of the human's path illuminated in the light of its sensory consciousness, we arrive at a false definition, we transform it into a mere physical problem. We must acknowledge it as a cosmic being, extending the earthly section of its path forwards and backwards in order to understand its true nature.

Now because in fact only the earthly section of our path is illuminated by our sensory self-awareness, the rest lies in darkness, therefore the foundation, the *ceterum censeo* [but I think] of all mystics, lies in the proposition: the self-awareness does not exhaust its object — in other words, there is a transcendental psychology. Anyone who proves this sentence, that we stand out above our self-awareness, and can exhaustively answer the question of how far we stand out — this will without doubt be the task of philosophy for the next century — will achieve for the puzzle of humanity what Schiaparelli achieved for the shooting star in that he proved that the section of its path illuminating the atmosphere is only a part of a greater cosmic curve. But if a few of these points are determined, then the form and position of the entire path can be calculated.

Because our sensory consciousness illuminates only the earthly section of our path lying between birth and death, the appearance must adhere to it as if birth were the beginning of existence, and death its end, that existence in addition is conferred by a foreign, mere earthly cause as a gift from outside us, and this appearance must consist for the earthly persons themselves then — if we as subjects have grasped with transcendental consciousness the voluntary conclusion — of diving into the earthly. The occult sciences teach now, however, the organising nature of the soul, and with that a pre-existence and post-existence is added to the earthly section of the path; they teach furthermore that we wander through these extended sections, which lie in the unconscious for us, with transcendental consciousness which we must place everywhere that the sensory consciousness stops or begins, on the other side of birth, as of death; they teach finally — indeed the production of genius already shows it — that this transcendental consciousness exists simultaneously with the sensory consciousness, even if it is hidden from the latter. Our entry into life thus occurs through an unconscious to us, but not in itself unconscious cause, and this cause does not lie outside us in the earthly conditions, but rather within us; it is a transcendental act of will. The external compulsion is only an appearance.

That all becomes yet clearer when we consider the reverse case that the accompaniment of an action by the sensory consciousness awakens the appearance of freedom, even if it happens under foreign compulsion. Spinoza expressed in a letter the deep words that a stone provided with consciousness, if it were thrown, would believe it was flying voluntarily. The sentence is perhaps literally true, for if all power — according to Schopenhauer and Wallace — is will, then that stone would, acknowledging its inner being, find in itself a will which drives it forward on the curve of the throw, just as it, arriving on the ground, would not find this will anymore, thus would consider its physical inertia to be a psychic one.

As the appearance of freedom can thus arise by virtue of the consciousness, so can the appearance of no freedom by virtue of the unconscious. Indeed even the content of our life which is determined by our own actions, on the one hand produced by the external conditions of existence, could yet on the other hand be determined transcendentally. Let us take for comparison the sailor mentioned at the start. If he had been given post-hypnotic commands before his abandonment on the island, which he would have had to carry out after months and years, then he would have carried them out at the correct time, and because it happened consciously, he would be caught in the deception of freedom. Even actions of our life could thus very well with respect to an individual or even historical mission follow likewise through post-hypnotic commands provided by the transcendental subject as hypnotist while we were in the state of sensory unconsciousness, but then be carried out with the appearance of freedom.

Kant said in his third antimony of pure reason, which concerns the contrast of necessity and freedom, that the changes in the world, including our actions, occur by necessity. Earthly considered, every action is the necessary product of motive and character, and Kant himself said that if we were to know exactly the empirical character of a person, we could conclude as to their actions in a specifically given situation with the same certainty with which we calculate an eclipse of the sun. Freedom, said Kant, is only to be encountered in the realm of the supersensory, of the intelligible, in the "thing in itself". If now, however, our earthly, empirical character is at base a supersensory being, a transcendental subject, then the supersensory freedom is that of an "ego in itself" and is to be thought of individually. In this respect the entry into life, which appears necessary to the consciousness because it confuses the conditions of life with their cause, would have to be a voluntary act of the subject, and since the empirical character itself is only the portrayal of the transcendental, the actions of our life are to be accounted for by the transcendental subject as free.

Thus that speculation of Kant, whose profundity Schopenhauer and Schelling admired so much, is now after 100 years explained by a fact of transcendental psychology, by the post-hypnotic command. The insight into the necessity of our actions is hence not in contradiction with our feeling of freedom and responsibility, but rather is compatible with it.

Autohypnosis and post-hypnotic commands are acknowledged phenomena and they spontaneously demand their utilisation in the above sense because they not only explain two philosophical puzzles, birth and the feeling of responsibility which exists despite necessity, but rather also certain otherwise inexplicable facts of experience, e.g. the rhythmic movements in our fate of which Hallenbach spoke in the "Magie der Zahlen" [Magic of Numbers], and the "intentionality in the fate of the individual" of which Schopenhauer spoke.

Were it now so, then it would also result from it that our earthly journey through life is arranged for our transcendental wellbeing, and that confers on us a transcendentally grounded resignation which achieves far more than the wisdom from hardship is capable of achieving.

At all points it thus repeats that transcendental psychology, because only in it is the solution to the puzzle of humanity to be found, brings reason into our existence, which considered materialistically merely from the earthly side appears as the greatest stupidity. For taken materialistically birth is only the result of a short pleasure which two individuals prepared in the well-known "égoisme à deux" [two-way egotism] at the expense of a third, the latter having to bear as penance for it the drudgery of life for a few decades. The question of whether such an égoisme à deux is morally right would then be answered in the negative; the question of whether there are duties of children towards parents, indeed whether there are any duties of any sort, would likewise be answered in the negative. All three answers, however, are to be answered in the affirmative from the standpoint of transcendental psychology, which therein shows its eminent significance too in practical respects.

The materialists, when they talk of morals, characteristically limit their investigation to the question of how morals have arisen; the other question, of whether morals are duties, remains unmentioned for good reason. In a merely material world which distinguishes itself only through greater extent from a retort, absolutely nothing is present in which a moral might be grounded; morals assume in accordance with their conception that world and human are not merely physical problems, but rather also metaphysical. When the materialist denies that and nevertheless preaches morals, he is just being illogical, which admittedly is never difficult for him.

Transcendental psychology by contrast is capable though not merely of preaching morals, but of founding them, because it teaches immortality and the dependence of the future condition on the use which we make in the here and now of our situation and abilities. That is, however, not only of practical interest, but even today of very topical interest; for in the process of decomposition of religion, morals have lost their old support, they would have to thus be gradually corroded on the present path. The present morals are the expression of the idealistic world views of the past which had their pedagogical value and fulfilled their aim, although the morals were insufficiently, indeed incorrectly founded on those world views. Morals would thus by necessity have to wither away if new infusions of blood were not flowing into them from a new idealistic world view.

This world view is only in the process of the beginnings of its formation, and hence our theoretical absentmindedness is reflected with regard to the moral problem again in the social absentmindedness with which modern humans form their lives. The one strives with Faustian drive for knowledge, but his fellow human does not concern him; the mind of the other is entirely directed at works of charity, but he disdains completely and utterly science and art. The one isolates himself in that he goes to the Trappists, or otherwise leads a more vegetative existence in simple tranquility; the other plunges himself into human life, chasing after the phantom of fame, strives thereby perhaps also after knowledge, but only because it confers power. Most finally chase only after sensory pleasures and after gold as the means of obtaining this pleasure. Because now with this striving by necessity many must fall too short — earth is just not a land of milk and honey — and because unavoidably unhealthy extremes of pauperism and wealth occur, in recent times the social question has thus emerged which expresses itself in people's heads quite variously, with the one as philosophical fantasy, with the other as blind destructive rage, or even as the smallest vanity and addiction to making people talk about it, like, for example, with the failed assassin Hödel*, or — to name a leader — with the vain Jew Lassalle† who dreamt of his victorious entrance into Berlin, with his beloved at his side. Anyone who is incapable of being a hero wants at least to become a Herostratos‡. With all these various tendencies in our society, everyone though believes they are doing the right thing, and have the corresponding world view, and right here the practical absent-mindedness shows itself as an effect of the theoretical.

Unfortunately even the legitimate components of this social movement are united in the view that reform is to be carried out in general on the basis of the materialistic world view. But this is absolutely a logical contradiction; for the more the theoretical materialism becomes a matter of conviction, the more it will practically be given full expression and thereby sharpen more and more the struggle for existence which socialism wants to alleviate. By external economic measures it can probably happen to a certain degree, but the most important thing always remains to alter humans in their inner substance so that philanthropy also exists without those external institutions which otherwise would always be felt by a fraction as a burdensome compulsion. Those socialists who in fact only have the moral tendency to help the poor and miserable sooner or later will arrive at the view that the so-

---

*   [Tr.: the anarchist Max Hödel (1857–1878) fired a revolver at Kaiser Wilhelm I, was arrested, tried and convicted of high treason, and executed.]

†   [Tr.: Ferdinand Lassalle (1825–1864), founder of the social democratic movement in Germany.]

‡   [Tr.: Herostratos set fire to the Temple of Artemis in Ephesus in 356 B.C. in order to become famous.]

cialism fused with the materialistic world view can never achieve this goal permanently, and that it is only achievable on the basis of a metaphysical world view. Such a one can, however, only be constructed in our century on the foundation of facts of experience, and for that reason it requires first the acknowledgement of transcendental psychology; it forms the actual entrance portal to the metaphysics.

There are very many among us who consider out culture optimistically blinded, seeing everything rosy and a considerable degree of morality already realised in our social conditions, hence they also cannot be convinced of the necessity of a new world view. But looked at closer the moral colouring of our culture dissolves into mere pretence, namely in the mere legality of action without moral conviction. This legality is kept upright with the educated by public opinion, with the uneducated by the authority of the state and the criminal code. Only what remains in our culture of morals after the withdrawal of that which is accounted for by both these factors is genuine and can be ascribed to inner conviction. Every time bestiality has come to the surface; thus with the "great" revolution, at which heads were carried around on pikes so that Paris sank down at one blow to the cultural level of Dahomey. Of a reduction in morals there can thus be no talk; only the compulsion was reduced which up to then legality had kept upright. Thus even with a new revolution, however, anarchists and nihilists bring the proof that we have our redskins in the midst of our civilisation, and the socialists of legitimate tendencies will achieve with difficulty the resisting of this society.

All that must be taken account of in an objective appraisal of our degree of morality, and shows how necessary the revival of belief in a metaphysics is, because only thus can morals be supported anew. But morals which shall not merely be commended outwardly, but rather grounded inwardly must themselves follow from the definition which the human receives in this new metaphysics. It thus also comes down here to the correct solution of the puzzle of humanity.

The grounding of morals is without doubt the hardest, but also the real task of philosophy; for the human is the highest fact of nature, and morals are its highest function. Instinctively we place it higher than cultural education. In the moral human we barely miss the cultural education, but genius without morals repels us. Stupidity excites sympathy or cheerfulness, wickedness excites outrage. The real touchstone of philosophical systems thus lies in whether they are capable of grounding morals.

The moral instinct is now, however, illogical if the human individuality only lies between cradle and grave. If only our visible section of the path had validity and we walked consciously towards our ceasing to exist, then we would be like those condemned to death, only our way to the place of execution would be somewhat longer, and the time we reached it uncertain. The law grants the condemned man for his last day the fulfillment of his bodily wishes. Thus it was even with the ancient Greeks. But we will assert this claim with neglect of preparation for the other side for the entire length of our life if as materialists we see death as annihilation.

Here it is shown that an analogous relationship exists for morals as for intelligence. The degree of intelligence is namely dependent on the development of the sense of time. The animal lives in the vivid present; it has no consciousness of time. The human in the condition of nomadic life is not much different; he draws no learning from the past and makes no preparations for the future. The educated human is thereby the highest earthly being because he takes past and future into account in his actions. The degree of development of the sense of time thus determines the biological level of a being, and is identical with the degree of development of reason. In this respect our entire culture is thus bound with respect to intelligence to the development of the consciousness of time. Without this the biological process would not have gotten beyond the animal.

As now the development of intelligence is tied to that of the earthly sense of time, so is the development of morals to that of the supernatural sense of time. It is absolutely possible when we recognise the earthly section of our path which is illuminated by sensory consciousness as merely part of a perhaps hyperbolic curve which we have travelled along. If in the increase in intelligence the earthly time might yet be encompassed so perfectly, towards past and future, then that can only ever be to the benefit of the intelligence, and become motive for striving after the welfare of our earthly person. But with that the conflict with morals sets in. We will only strive for the welfare of our entire, our real being when our consciousness of time goes beyond earthly existence and the metaphysical nature of humanity is acknowledged again. The moral human will also be taken up by the increase of this sense of time and the elevation of humanity bound up with it.

Having us acknowledge this goal is the task of transcendental psychology. It teaches that the human is the materialisation of a transcendental subject, the embodiment of a supersensory being. As an essential part of nature the human is surely the epitome of what all of nature seems to be, which does not arise from nothing, but rather can only be the materialisation of an invisible world. So thought the mystics*. The Bible calls this materialisation of our invisible being "expulsion from paradise". We can retain the myth, only we will interpret in the sense of the occult sciences, as Philo, Origen, the cabbalists, Plotinus and Plato did in his idealist philosophy. Paradise *precedes* birth, and is the pre-existence. The fall from grace does not first follow birth, rather it *is* the earthly birth. It coincides with the expulsion from paradise, that is, through birth our transcendental existence becomes unconscious to us. The "coats of skins" with which God clothed the fallen humans† are the earthly bodies of which they were ashamed when they recognised them, whereas they were not ashamed of the previous nakedness of their etheric bodies. Through the fall from grace, so says the Bible, death came into the world. Certainly, for materialisation is on account of the transience of all matter only temporal, and dematerialisation, death, must follow it. For just that reason we should use life to obtain such goods which outlast death. The programme of our life conduct is determined by the knowledge that we are capable of development beyond death.

This definition of the "fall from grace" will certainly not please the theologians who have no idea of the esoteric side to

---

*   Louis-Claude de Saint-Martin, Tableau naturel des rapports qui existent entre Dieu, l'homme et l'univers (Lyon, 1782), 25–26.

†   Genesis 3:21.

their own dogmas; but the myth understood esoterically is true. If you insist by contrast on the literal exoteric interpretation of the dogmas, then they will become untenable on the level of scientific knowledge, and all efforts of the theologians cannot then hinder that the number of unbelievers constantly grows. Just in that exists the truth of every profound myth, that it grows at each level of knowledge into a different interpretation without becoming obsolete; when the naive interpretation has become untenable, a deeper one appears. Understood esoterically the story of Adam in our children's catechism thus also receives an element of truth.

The church will certainly not be happy with such concessions, and hence its conflict with the modern mysticism is also not to be avoided, and it will perhaps soon be settled. This conflict is to be regretted in so far as the actual enemy of humanity and an ideal culture being materialism, for whose combatting all should be united who, in whatever form, believe in a metaphysics. But it would be naive to hope for that from a church which since time immemorial has persecuted all those of a different faith, even if their faith only differed from the church by a shade. It has conducted this struggle since time immemorial with all the means standing at its current command, with fire and sword, as long as it was mighty, and conducts it still today, when it has lost its might, with milder means.

Apart from that, it cannot for a moment be doubtful to the modern mysticism on which side the victory will be in the coming conflict. The church will never let go of the claim that its dogmas are revelations which may not be quibbled over, but rather must simply be believed, and indeed in the exoteric sense. To get through with these demands, however, they have no chance. You do not understand our century if you do not want to see that humanity has outgrown the leash of faith, and can no longer be led by it. The century of the natural sciences does not want to believe anymore, but rather to know. The transition is admittedly not so easy, and it must temporarily have severe disadvantages as a result; but considered in itself it is a gratifying phenomenon when humanity feels the need to be raised from the level of faith to the higher one of knowledge. The truth can only obtain power by it if it is not merely believed but rather is known, and the knowing human himself stands higher than the believing one. The loss of belief, when it grasps the masses even before the replacement is there, is certainly regrettable, but only for the periods of transition. If our eyes could see out over these periods, then the jeremiads over the modern unbelief would fall silent.

At present it is certainly precisely our problem of immortality which suffers the worst under the modern unbelief. The conviction of the inadequacy of the previous proofs is already a mass phenomenon, and for as long as the stronger, indeed completely irreproachable proofs of immortality do not penetrate into the masses, they will throw the baby out with the bath water and fill it up in the meantime with materialism. Thus we see today that in worker circles Büchner's "Kraft und Stoff" [Force and Matter] belongs amongst the most read books. Therein lies indisputably a great danger; you are yourself conscious of, and the church understands how to make capital from this fearful mood. As a means for extinguishing the petrol they offer the state holy water. Phenomena, like the Prussian draft school reform, are explained by this situation. You want to start with the schools in order to make the masses faithful again; you thus believe you can simply pass over the characteristic signature of our century which wants to progress from faith to knowledge. The masses shall become faithful again, and to this end science shall subordinate itself to faith. With this enormous claim the church has previously only achieved the constant increase of the unbelief, and it is obvious that it *can* achieve nothing else from it even in the future. If the word evolution applies to history just as much as to biology, then a church which raises the *inability* to evolve of religion and the eternal application of their dogmas in a literal sense to a principle can only lose more and more in power. The church cannot win over a science which contrasts to the should believe the want to know. Only such a metaphysics has prospects of finding acceptance with the masses and ousting materialism from those who acknowledge the principle of the spiritual/intellectual development of humanity, and only it is capable of giving the metaphysical ideas the foundation of facts of experience. Because the natural sciences have satisfied this demand, have penetrated into the masses, and from now on these masses will also raise this demand against every metaphysics. In short, humanity outgrows the belief in revelation more and more, speculative metaphysics always becomes caviar for the people, and the masses could only be converted to such a metaphysics as has stripped off the disadvantages of dogmatism and has won the advantages of scientific knowledge.

This advantage is now offered to that world view which advances on facts based on the occult sciences, advancing its feelers as far as the area of metaphysics. It is therefore clear that the modern mysticism, when its conflict with the church will take place, has every prospect of winning over the masses. Even in our circles of workers the need for education is already stirring. They know very well that knowledge is power, indeed they are convinced that a lasting victory can only ever fall to that party which represents the truth. Now the church comes and claims that just it is in possession of the truth and offers — dogmas in which it becomes with increasing knowledge ever more difficult to believe, in which the Latin students are already beginning to doubt, and which the student throws over board down to the last bit. Modern mysticism does the exact opposite of that. It does not demand that you believe, but rather that you investigate; it offers facts instead of dogmas; it offers a world view which, with increasing study, becomes more and more plausible and finally turns into firm scientific conviction, into knowledge. It does not have to fear investigation, but rather demands it. Indeed still more; it demands the experiment, and knows definitely that anyone who follows this advice must become a convinced adherent of this new world view. Such a world view must unavoidably penetrate more and more into the masses. The church is not a match for such an opponent; it, demanding the "sacrifice of the mind", is not able to compete against a world view which demands the use of the mind, indeed one which invites exact experiment, and of which ever new proofs are expected.

Now what is more is that the state and a church intent on its real welfare, on its ability to live, would have every cause to support such a movement which will sweep away materialism and reinvigorate the faith in metaphysics. If such a metaphysics moreover agrees with religion on such an essential point as immortality and delivers proofs for it, while the church does not dispose of any such, then indeed for religion itself a prize is let go, against which it does not come into consideration when other components of the Catholic or Protestant orthodoxy should enter the breach.

Humanity will thus return to faith in metaphysics, but not by drumming dogmas into children's heads, but rather by presenting facts to adults for examination. The church is not succeeding, despite its magnificent apparatus, in preserving its believers, but still less have its papal bulls and bishopric pastoral letters succeeded even in converting back just *one* materialist; modern mysticism by contrast, merely because it stands on the side of the facts, sees the number of its adherents constantly grow, and has already up to now done enormous harm to materialism.

Thus the theory of souls then proves to be, in that it takes transcendental psychology into account, of quite wide-ranging importance in practical respects. But as a theory it not only solves the puzzle of humanity to a degree previously never achieved, but also partly solves the puzzle of the world; the point of the world becomes partly transparent to us, and we recognise that the world is a nursery for spirits which through the expulsion from the transcendental paradise may perhaps be furthered more than in the paradise itself.

Diagram for Explaining the Human from

The Human

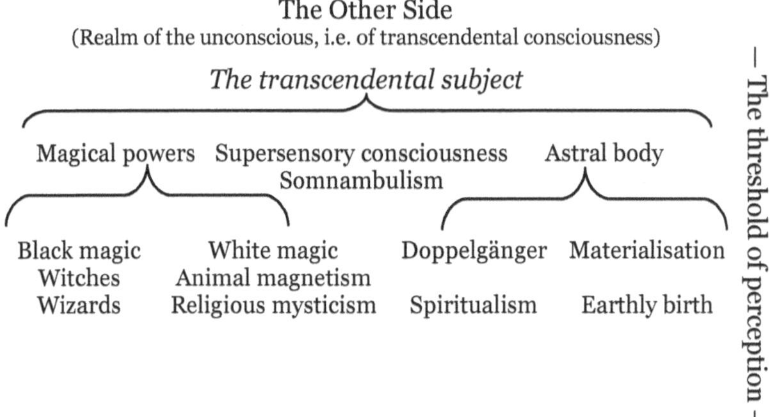

Explanation

Humans live simultaneously on the other side as transcendental subjects and in the here and now as earthly humans. Both ways of existence are different in respect to forms of cognition and ways of action. The other side and the here and now are not spatially separate, but rather they are divided only by the threshold of perception, accordingly the sensory consciousness only encompasses the earthly existence. The other side is the here and now viewed differently. A monistic explanation of the earthly human, according to body and spirit, demands proof of the identity of the thinking and organising principle in a transcendental subject, wherewith at the same time the foundation is obtained for the occult sciences. The powers and abilities of the transcendental subject, in so far as they become conscious to us by way of exception in the here and now (somnambulism) and from the other side crossing over into the here and now (spiritualism), form the object of the occult sciences. That proof of identity is also essential for the understanding of this. But this proof, in order to be safe against materialistic objections, can for the sceptical reader be obtained most expediently from the mentioned phenomena which belong to the area of aesthetics and technology.

the Standpoint of the Occult Sciences

The Human

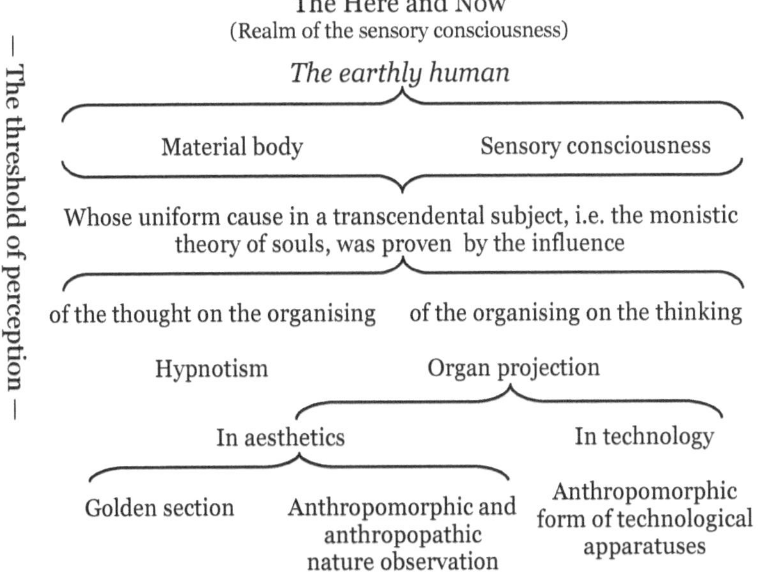